THE EIGHT BEST RETIREM ꞈND
CHIANG MAI, KOH Sꓱ
HUA HIN, KRABI, Cꞁ

GERꓕ

CW01475098

Copyright

THE EIGHT BEST RETIREMENT
LOCATIONS IN THAILAND
CHIANG MAI, KOH SAMUI, BANGKOK, PHUKET,
HUA HIN, KRABI, CHIANG RAI AND PATTAYA

1st edition 2024
Published independently by Gerald Hogg

Copyright © Gerald Hogg 2024

A CIP catalogue record for this title is available from the British Library.
The information provided within this book is for general informational purposes only. While we try to keep the information up-to-date and correct, there are no representations or warranties, express or implied, about the completeness, accuracy, reliability, suitability or availability concerning the information, products, services, or related graphics contained in this book for any purpose. Any use of this information is at your own risk so do your own research.

TABLE OF CONTENTS

THE RETIREES TRAVEL GUIDE SERIES

FACTS ABOUT THAILAND

Capitol...Bangkok

Population...72 million (21st most populace in the world)

Land Area...513,120 square meters

Provinces...76

Government...Democratic Constitutional Monarchy

Currency...Thai Baht.

Language...Thai but English is widely spoken in most tourist towns

Climate...Tropical Climate

Power voltage...220 volts. Plugs A & C

Religion...92.5% Buddhist, 5.4 % Muslim, and 1.2 % Christian.

Time Zone...UTC+7

Driving Side...Left

Country Phone Code...+66

Police, Fire and Ambulance ...#1719

Thailand is the only Southeast Asian country that was never colonized by a European country

One-tenth of the entire population of Thailand lives in Bangkok

There are more than 35,000 temples in Thailand.

Thailand was once known as Siam and is the country where Siamese cats originated.

The first Siamese twins were born in Siam (now Thailand) in 1811 and were conjoined from birth until they died when they were 63

INTRODUCTION

In my book *THE RETIRE in THAILAND HANDBOOK 2023...THE NEXT SIX YEARS* I wrote about the eight best places to live or retire in Thailand. This was just a summary and was not an in-depth account. This book is a comprehensive look at those same eight towns that I consider to be the best areas for expats to live in Thailand. Of course, where you may want to live in this fascinating and diverse country will depend on your outlook on life, hobbies and the lifestyle that you want to achieve in your new country and there are many more towns that might tick the boxes for where you may want to live These are just my personal favourites, places that I have either lived in or spent a considerable amount of time in. So, before you decide where is the best place for you to live, do your own research because even though places like Udon Thani, Khon Kaen and Khao Nakhon Ratchasima are not places that I would consider for my needs in retirement they could be more suited to what you are looking for when looking for a place to call home.

Thailand is one of the most popular countries for retirees from all around the world, and there are a lot of reasons why that is so. For pennies in the pound, you get a tropical climate, beautiful palm-fringed islands, friendly smiling people, and affordable high-quality medical care. A country where Buddhist monks, golden beaches, palm trees, monkeys and elephants become part of your everyday life. The problem with Thailand is you're spoilt for choice. So where do you start to look for the best place to live or to spend your golden years? As I said this will depend on your personal choice of what you are looking to achieve in retirement. For instance, I absolutely love Chiang Mai. I love the people as they seem much friendlier than many other places I have visited in Thailand. The climate is nicer with cooler weather. It has a slower pace of life; the surrounding countryside is so green and best of all it's one of the cheapest places to live in Thailand. The problem for me is it's too far from the coast. Working at sea for most of my life I have always had a love of the sea and can't see myself ever wanting to live away from the coast as all of the places that I have ever lived have been near the sea. For that reason and that reason alone, I could never live in Chiang Mai, but I holiday there as often as possible. There are many considerations you will have to take into account before you can decide where the best place in Thailand is *"RIGHT FOR YOU"* to retire.

If you're like me and love beaches then deciding where to live is going to be a very hard choice for you as Thailand is surrounded by some of the most magnificent beaches and tropical islands in the world. If you love the quiet and solitude of country life then the same applies, there are just so many wonderful rural places to choose from. If you love city life, culture and nightlife then Bangkok is probably the place for you. It's also just over a two-and-a-half-hour drive to Pattaya or a beautiful two-and-a-half-hour ferry ride to Koh Samet should you also like the beach life. Currently, I am living in Hua Hin which is also a beautiful coastal town and only a couple of hours' drive from Bangkok and the city is very central to the rest of Thailand. But I am often torn between Hua Hin and my other favourite place in Thailand Koh Samui.

Unless you have been to Thailand many times before and you have already chosen the place you may soon be calling home, you will need to get lots of videos and books and look on the internet to ensure that you are choosing the right place to spend the rest of your life. Take a look at my YouTube channel, *Thailand My Land* and other YouTube channels relating to Thailand, there are thousands of them to view to help you find the best regions in Thailand that tick most of the boxes for you. Make a wish list, and then visit those places when you arrive to make your decision. There really is no rush. You have retired so take your time. Spend months or even years looking around until you find the place that is just right for you.

My eight favourite places for retirees in Thailand in no particular order are:

- Chiang Mai
- Koh Samui
- Bangkok
- Phuket
- Hua Hin
- Krabi
- Chiang Rai
- Pattaya

These are my favourite places that tick most of the boxes for my own personal lifestyle but there are many more areas of

Thailand that many ex-pats call home that may be a good fit for you such as Kohn Kaen, Nakhon Ratchasima, Udon Thani, Phitsanoluk, Chumphon and Koh Lak the list is endless so do your research for where is the right place for your lifestyle.

Some of the things you will need to keep in mind when looking for a new place to call home are; what kind of facilities are in the area? If you love golf but the nearest golf course is a three-hour drive away, then it's probably not the place for you. If you hate busy places and lots of people then Bangkok, Phuket or Pattaya should be crossed off your list. If you're into scuba diving in the ocean then don't even consider Chiang Mai or Chiang Rai as the nearest ocean is about a 13-hour drive away. This is where the research before you leave home, is invaluable. It can save you time and money by filtering out the places that don't tick the boxes. This will allow you to spend more time in the places on your wish list to help you make that important decision of where you want to live in your retirement.

Gerald Hogg
Hua Hin
January 2024

CHIANG MAI

CHAPTER ONE

CHIANG MAI

Chiang Mai is located in the upper northern area of Thailand. The name Chiang Mai translates to New City yet the city is over 700 years old and was founded as the capital of the Lanna Kingdom at the end of the 13th century when the town quickly became a major trading post between southern China, Burma which is Myanmar today and Lan Xang which is now called Laos. This prominence made Chiang Mai a target of attacks by neighbouring armies and the city finally fell to the invaders from Burma in 1558. In 1774 the king of Siam, King Taksin drove out the Burmese, and Chiang Mai retained a degree of independence from Bangkok until the late 19th century. Finally, in 1932 the Chiang Mai area officially became a province of Siam and in 1949 the country changed its name from Siam to Thailand, though many local people from Chiang Mai still proudly display their ties to the old Lanna Kingdom. Today Chiang Mai is a vibrant mixture of a modern city mixed with hundreds of years of history. Chiang Mai is the largest city in northern Thailand and the third largest city in Thailand after the capital of Thailand, Bangkok and Nakhon Ratchasima. The city is located on the Ping River which is the major tributary of the Chao Phraya River. The older part of the town still retains the 18th-century walled settlement and also many of the ruins from the 13th and 14th centuries. There are so many Temples in Chiang Mai and the surrounding area that it is said that if you visited one every day it would take you about ten months to see them all. Chiang Mai lies 700 km north of Bangkok and is surrounded by mountains where you will find colourful hill tribes including the Hmong, Lahu, Akha, Palong, Mien, Lisu, and Lawa, and of course, the famous Karen or the Long Neck Tribe as they are more commonly known. If you love to play golf the Chiang Mai area is home to fourteen outstanding golf courses all with stunning natural scenery. There are many festivals held every year in Chiang Mai. The two main ones are the Thai New Year, or Songkran which is a water festival in April and Loy Krathong in November, neither of which should not be missed.

SOME FACTS ABOUT CHIANG MAI

- Population of Chiang Mai city: 1.2 million
- Chiang Mai Province has a population of 1.8 million
- Chiang Mai has a tropical savanna climate with warm to hot weather year-round, though nighttime conditions during the dry season can be cool and much lower than the daytime highs.
- Chiang Mai lies approximately 700 kilometres north of Bangkok and is 250 kilometres south of the Myanmar border.
- Chiangmai is the largest city in northern Thailand, the capital of Chiang Mai province and the third largest city in Thailand after Bangkok and Nakhon Ratchasima.
- There are an estimated 25,000 foreign expats living in Chiang Mai.
- Chiang Mai dates back to 1296 when it was founded as the new capital of the Lanna Kingdom.
- The name of Chiang Mai means *New City* and was named when it succeeded its sister city Chiang Rai as the Lanna capital.
- Chiang Mai is home to Thailand's highest mountain, Doi Inthanon.
- Chiang Mai province is home to the Hill tribes such as the Karen Long Neck Tribe who originated in Burma before migrating to Thailand in the 17th century other Hill tribes include the Hmong, Akha, Mien, Lahu, Lisu and Palaung.
- Chiang Mai is the second most visited area in Thailand after Bangkok.
- Chiang Mai Province is home to over 50 elephant sanctuaries. With Thailand's estimated population of elephants being about 2,700 and worldwide an estimated 50,000 Asian elephants, the sanctuaries are crucial for their survival.

- The locals speak Thai, but many of the descendants of the original settlers often communicate with each other in the Lanna language.
- Chiang Mai is the world's capital of digital nomads due to its low cost of living and its high-speed Internet.
- There are over 300 Buddhist temples in the province.

THE WEATHER IN CHIANG MAI

One of the main reasons that expats choose to live in Chiang Mai is the weather. November to February is the best time of year with clear blue skies and temperatures around the 25°c mark with low humidity. The rest of the year averages around 30°c. The rainy season is from May until October when it often rains twice a day in sometimes monsoon-type conditions. When the rain clears, it just highlights the greenness of the area and makes Chiang Mai even more beautiful. Most people agree that Chiang Mai has the best climate in Thailand if not the best in South East Asia. One big problem Chiang Mai does have is the air pollution that happens every year between November and February caused by the many farmers in the area burning off their fields to prepare for the next season's crops. Depending on the wind and rain during that time the area has been known to be one of the worst in the world for air pollution with the smoke and burnt crop particles rising into the air and hanging over the city making the air sometimes unbreathable during those months.

If you have breathing or respiratory problems Chiang Mai may not be a good place for you to be during those months but if you are a retiree without those health problems or want to escape the city during those months to Koh Samui, Krabi or other more breathable areas in Thailand, but your someone who prefers a cooler climate the rest of the year then Chiang Mai could be the place for you. Here are some other reasons why Chiang Mai could be the place for you to retire.

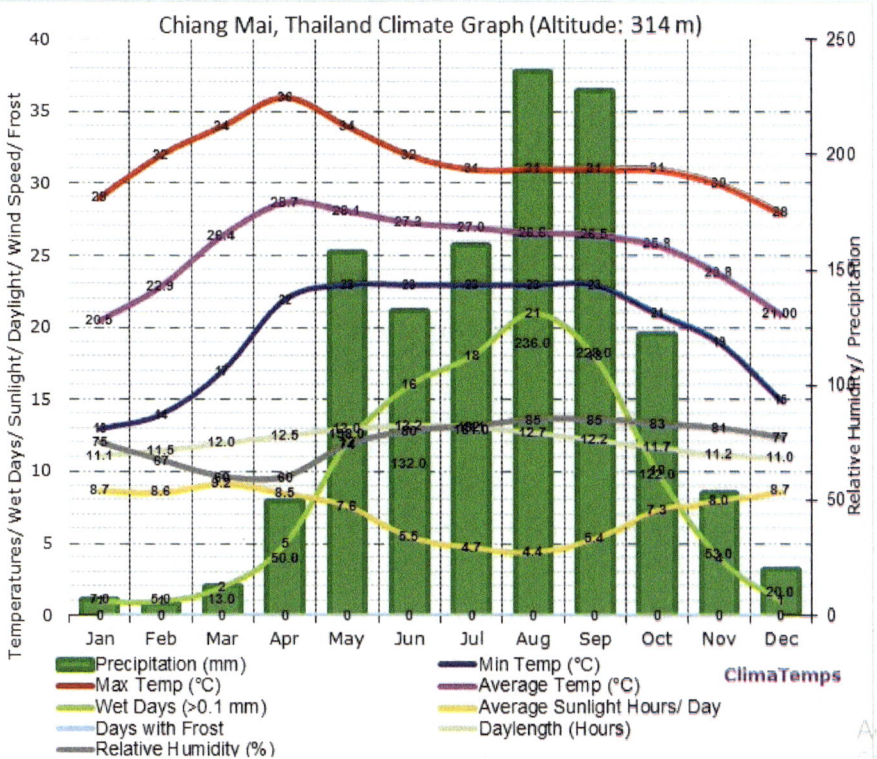

Chiang Mai, Thailand Climate Graph (Altitude: 314 m)

Courtesy of www. travelfish .org

THE COST OF LIVING IN CHIANG MAI

Summary of cost of living in Chiang Mai, Thailand:

A family of four estimated monthly costs are 63,363.8฿ without rent.
A single person's estimated monthly costs are 17,836.2฿ without rent.
Chiang Mai is 23.9% less expensive than Bangkok
Rent in Chiang Mai is, on average, 47.4% lower than in Bangkok.

A big plus for living in Chiang Mai is the affordable cost of living. And the city has a lot more to offer, baht for baht than most other cities and towns in Thailand. You can eat out at street stalls or in shopping malls for ridiculously low prices. The cost of renting and buying property continues to be one of the lowest-priced areas in Thailand. You need to take into account that if you want to regularly travel throughout Thailand, Chiang Mai being in Northern Thailand and close to the Laos border is a long way from Bangkok and the tropical islands and beaches in the southern areas of Thailand. For instance, to drive from Chiang Mai to Phuket is a 22-hour non-stop drive. Chiang Mai does have an international airport, so if flying not driving is your thing, then it shouldn't make any difference to you. The overall cost of living here would depend on your own personal lifestyle. Nonetheless, many ex-pats live comfortably in Chiang Mai for less than US$1000 a month. If you are looking to live more luxurious in Chiang Mai, then a budget of $1500 would allow you a decent standard of living. Over recent years, Chiang Mai has become a popular destination for many ex-pats who are looking to retire or live in a more economical country than the one that they grew up in. One of the main reasons for that is Chiang Mai has a more relaxed feel than places like Bangkok, Pattaya and Phuket while at the same time having everything you need to live a good life such as cinemas, shopping centres, exciting nightlife and different food options from 5-star dining to the thousands of food stalls that are featured all around the city.

✗ Restaurants

Meal, Inexpensive Restaurant	62.50 ฿
Meal for 2 People, Mid-range Restaurant, Three-course	560.00 ฿
McMeal at McDonalds (or Equivalent Combo Meal)	200.00 ฿
Domestic Beer (0.5 liter draught)	72.50 ฿
Imported Beer (0.33 liter bottle)	120.00 ฿
Cappuccino (regular)	54.55 ฿
Coke/Pepsi (0.33 liter bottle)	18.39 ฿
Water (0.33 liter bottle)	11.00 ฿

☵ Markets

Milk (regular), (1 liter)	54.47 ฿
Loaf of Fresh White Bread (500g)	47.83 ฿
Rice (white), (1kg)	41.12 ฿
Eggs (regular) (12)	66.00 ฿
Local Cheese (1kg)	487.50 ฿
Chicken Fillets (1kg)	79.27 ฿
Beef Round (1kg) (or Equivalent Back Leg Red Meat)	407.50 ฿
Apples (1kg)	91.62 ฿
Banana (1kg)	42.00 ฿
Oranges (1kg)	48.75 ฿
Tomato (1kg)	60.62 ฿
Potato (1kg)	45.00 ฿
Onion (1kg)	35.00 ฿
Lettuce (1 head)	30.00 ฿
Water (1.5 liter bottle)	16.44 ฿
Bottle of Wine (Mid-Range)	500.00 ฿
Domestic Beer (0.5 liter bottle)	62.17 ฿
Imported Beer (0.33 liter bottle)	107.78 ฿
Cigarettes 20 Pack (Marlboro)	140.00 ฿

🚗 Transportation

One-way Ticket (Local Transport)	30.00 ฿
Monthly Pass (Regular Price)	800.00 ฿
Taxi Start (Normal Tariff)	40.00 ฿
Taxi 1km (Normal Tariff)	45.00 ฿
Taxi 1hour Waiting (Normal Tariff)	100.00 ฿
Gasoline (1 liter)	41.25 ฿
Volkswagen Golf 1.4 90 KW Trendline (Or Equivalent New Car)	725,000.00 ฿
Toyota Corolla Sedan 1.6l 97kW Comfort (Or Equivalent New Car)	801,666.67 ฿

🛁 Utilities (Monthly)

Basic (Electricity, Heating, Cooling, Water, Garbage) for 85m2 Apartment	1,851.13 ฿
Mobile Phone Monthly Plan with Calls and 10GB+ Data	477.55 ฿
Internet (60 Mbps or More, Unlimited Data, Cable/ADSL)	676.24 ฿

🚲 Sports And Leisure

Fitness Club, Monthly Fee for 1 Adult	1,255.56 ฿
Tennis Court Rent (1 Hour on Weekend)	233.33 ฿
Cinema, International Release, 1 Seat	205.00 ฿

🛒 Childcare

Preschool (or Kindergarten), Full Day, Private, Monthly for 1 Child	15,833.33 ฿
International Primary School, Yearly for 1 Child	394,888.89 ฿

👕 Clothing And Shoes

1 Pair of Jeans (Levis 501 Or Similar)	1,800.00 ฿
1 Summer Dress in a Chain Store (Zara, H&M, ...)	1,058.33 ฿
1 Pair of Nike Running Shoes (Mid-Range)	3,000.00 ฿
1 Pair of Men Leather Business Shoes	2,200.00 ฿

🛏 Rent Per Month

Apartment (1 bedroom) in City Centre	14,333.33 ฿
Apartment (1 bedroom) Outside of Centre	7,911.76 ฿
Apartment (3 bedrooms) in City Centre	27,000.00 ฿
Apartment (3 bedrooms) Outside of Centre	16,000.00 ฿

🏢 Buy Apartment Price

Price per Square Meter to Buy Apartment in City Centre	60,600.00 ฿
Price per Square Meter to Buy Apartment Outside of Centre	33,250.00 ฿

Courtesy of www.numbeo.com
THE FRIENDLY PEOPLE OF CHIANG MAI

Thailand is known as the land of smiles, though the smiles have faded a little since COVID-19 first arrived in January 2020. I still believe that whoever coined the phrase Land of Smiles must have been visiting Chiang Mai at the time. Because of its northern location, Chiang Mai is influenced by the Lanna people. You will find the Lanna influence everywhere you go in Chiang Mai their art, costumes, music, food, culture and ancestry are seen throughout the city. Chiang Mai is situated in the mountainous area of northwest Thailand and is the home of Doi Inthanon; the mountain with the highest elevation in the country. The mountain areas have been home to many different groups of hill tribes or Chao Khao who migrated from places like Yunan in China, Northern Burma, Laos and Tibet over the years. Chao Khao translates to Mountain people. It is estimated that there are 312,000 hill tribe people living within the Chiang Mai Province, and each of the tribes has their own unique customs, culture and language.

Overall, the people in Chiang Mai are friendly, helpful and honest. I am not saying that other areas of Thailand are not friendly, helpful or honest; in fact, nothing could be further from the truth. It's just that the people of Chiang Mai seem to go out of their way to help and don't have the mentality of getting what they can out of the farang like in some of the more touristy beach towns. They are a very proud people and know that their traditions and customs are different from the rest of Thailand. They want tourists and ex-pats who visit Chiang Mai to go back home and tell their friends and family about Chiang Mai, they love the fact that they are seen as the nicest people in Thailand.

WHAT DOES CHIANG MAI OFFER FOR EXPATS LIVING THERE?

Chiang Mai with an estimated 30,000 expats living here is reported to be the third largest expat community in Thailand after Bangkok and Pattaya, with many of them being retirees. This is probably because of the cheaper cost of living, and the more agreeable climate. There are both good and bad with coming to Thailand and joining expat clubs but the good far outweighs the bad. The good elements include social networking with people similar to you. You're a long way from home and you're probably going to miss it, especially when you first arrive after leaving your family and friends. Mixing with other people, who have been in the same position as you are, can help you feel less homesick, and help you put down roots quicker. They have been in your shoes and most will want to help you settle in. Many of them have lived in Thailand for many years and have a wealth of knowledge of the area and Thailand in general. They know the best ways to find a property, where to rent a vehicle, the best places to shop, where to get a haircut, and the cheapest or the best restaurants to go to. They can save you a lot of time and money because of their expertise in all things Thai that they have learnt by living here. Some of the expat clubs organise tennis tournaments, golf, cricket, theme dinners, social tours in Thailand and South East Asia and other sporting and social events. If you're a single male or single female then you will find lots of single friends of both sexes to mix with and hopefully become friends with, this makes it a lot easier going out socialising rather than going out alone.

One of the not-so-good reasons for mixing too much with other expats is that you sometimes forget about making friends with Thais. Not intentionally but sometimes because of the language barrier and because you don't spend a lot of time socialising with Thais, you sometimes forget about making friends with them and stick with your own compadres. One of the things I love about travelling is meeting the locals and seeing how their lives are different from mine. You will also find that when befriending local Thais, they will help you assimilate into their country and culture. You will find out where they shop and the best places to visit that other people might not even hear about which can save you a lot of money. I have found that Thais love to talk to us farang and find out about our lives. Many Thais are just shy or don't believe their English is good enough to communicate. If you take the time to talk with them and try to help them understand you and if you can learn some of their language, you will be surprised how much they appreciate talking to you and learning about your country and your life. Thais also have a great sense of humour once you get past the language barrier.

The only other thing that I am hesitant about in the expat community is you can get stuck in a rut. Many expats retire here for the cheap food, drinks and the girls. Nothing wrong with that if that's how you want to live your life it's probably a great way to live if that's all you want out of life. The problem as I see it is, you don't do anything else with your life in this beautiful country and fantastic area of South East Asia. Here in the area of Hua Hin where I am living, when I am driving on my way to the beach or the shops or out walking, I pass lots of bars. Aussie bars, British bars, Swiss bars, German bars...all kinds of bars. What I have noticed is that I see the same faces sitting in the same seats most days at different times of the day. Whether they have been there all day or left and came back later I have no way of knowing. I sometimes have a couple of beers in the Brit bar or the Aussie bar and listen to the talk around the bar. A lot of the talk I hear is about home and the lives they left behind and what great lives they have now, though you also get the grumpy ones who run Thailand down and complain about everything here. I often feel like saying, *"No one is making you stay here if it's that bad go back to the life you had in the old country"*, but for my sanity, I bite my tongue and usually head for the beach. For me going to the same bar every day, sitting in the same seat talking to the same person next to you is not my idea of spending a great retirement in Thailand. In the end, it will be up to you how you want to live your new life in Thailand and as long as you are happy with how you live your life that's all that matters.

*See Useful Website pages at the end of

this book for expat club links

PLACES TO GO AND THINGS TO DO IN CHIANG MAI

WAT PHRA THAT DOI SUTHEP.

It is said that if you visited one temple a day in Chiang Mai Province it would take you nearly a year to see them all. But the most famous attraction and temple in all of Chiang Mai is Wat Doi Suthep. It is what Buckingham Palace is to London. The Statue of Liberty is to New York and the Eifel Tower is to Paris, it is top of every tourist's to-do list when visiting Chiang Mai. The Doi Suthep Mountain lies about 12 kilometres outside of Chiang Mai and on top of the mountain sits Wat Phra That Doi Suthep at an elevation of 1,073 meters with sweeping panoramic views across Chiang Mai and the surrounding countryside.

Legend has it that a white elephant, carrying a bone believed to be from Buddha, suddenly died on top of the mountain. This was taken as a spiritual sign, leading local people to build a sacred temple in the same spot where the elephant died and the temple has been there since 1383. You climb the 306 steps to the top, with the steps bordered by snake-like carvings known as a Naga staircase. If you're not feeling energetic enough to tackle the steps on the way up you can take a cable car to the top but it is a lot easier coming down the stairs and it's an exhilarating walk down if you are able to do so.

CHIANG MAI OLD CITY.

Construction on what is now Chiang Mai Old City began in 1296. The site was chosen as an alternative to the capital city of Chiang Rai at the time which was located in an area prone to flooding. This move proved to be a good one as the old capital was eventually buried in a mudslide when the course of the Ping River shifted. One of the main features of Chiang Mai Old City today is the wall that circles it and the two gates, each one designed and built with a specific purpose in mind. The most important gate, Chang Puak Gate, in the north wall was reserved for royalty during state visits and events. Today the walled, moated Old City is Chiang Mai's cultural heart, as within its walls are century-old temple compounds like Wat Phra Singh, known for its Lion Buddha statue, and Wat Chedi Luang, with a huge reconstructed pagoda.

THE LANNA FOLKLIFE MUSEUM.

The Lanna Folklife Museum is actually three museums combined. They are dedicated to the culture of Northern Thailand and are full of exhibitions about the lives, history and culture of the Lanna people of northern Thailand. The museum offers a lot of information about the city's history in English, Thai and Chinese. The museum contains Buddhist art, ceremonial utensils, handicrafts, sculptures, ceramics and paintings of the Lanna culture which contains exhibits on religious ritual artefacts dating back to the Lanna period, mural paintings, Buddhist relics, lacquerware, woven basketry, traditional musical instruments.

WAROROT MARKET.

Probably the best market that is open in the daytime is Warorot Market and it is also the largest market in the city. It is known as Warorot Market, but the Warorot Market is one of three markets within this sprawling complex the other two are the Ton Lam Yai and the Nawarat Markets. You can find just about everything at the market such as vegetables, fruit, meat, clothing, jewellery, souvenirs and many other things. The market sits next to the Ping River east of the old town and right next to Chinatown and the market is very popular among locals. When leaving the market along the side streets you will find a lot of Thai handicraft goods made by the local Hill Tribe people and again at much cheaper prices than anywhere else.

WAT CHEDI LUANG.

Known as the Temple of the Big Stupa, Wat Chedi Luang lies in the ruins of an ancient temple situated in the centre of Chaing Mai. The temple grounds at Wat Chedi Luang are home to several important buildings and Buddha images, but it is the ancient chedi or pagoda at the rear of the complex that is the most striking feature of Wat Chedi Luang. The temple was once the home to the famous Emerald Buddha, the holiest religious object in all of Thailand that now has pride of place in Wat Phra Kaeo in Bangkok. The pagoda was originally built in 1391 but was reconstructed nearly a century later to become the tallest building in what was then the Lanna kingdom. Wat Chedi Luang is also home to the City Pillar, known in Thailand as Inthakin. Every year in May, the Inthakin Festival is held to honour the pillar which is believed by local people to protect the city. An old gum tree is located adjacent to the white shrine that holds the City Pillar and legend has it that as long as the tree stands Chiang Mai will survive and prosper.

DOI INTHANON NATIONAL PARK.

Doi Inthanon is one of the most popular national parks in Thailand. It is famous for its waterfalls, walking trails, remote villages, viewpoints, sunrise and sunset watching, birdwatching and the all-year-round cooler weather due to its high elevation. The main park entrance is about 70 km southwest of Chiang Mai city and is known as "The Roof of Thailand". The national park covers an area of 482 square kilometres and the highest peak is Doi Inthanon Mountain which is the highest mountain

24

in the whole of Thailand. The park is named in honour of King Inthawichayanon, one of the last Lanna kings of Chiang Mai, who was concerned about the forests in the north of Thailand and wanted to preserve them. After his death, his remains were placed in the park as he ordered and the forest was renamed to Doi Inthanon.

It's a two-hour drive west of Chiang Mai but it is well worth the drive and Doi Inthanon National Park should not be missed if you like the great outdoors. There is accommodation within the national park so if you don't fancy a 4-hour drive in one day you can stay the night and see a magnificent sunset that evening and then get up the next morning to witness the sun rise over the mountains before heading back to Chiang Mai. There are many restaurants and coffee shops within the park.

DOI SUTHEP-PUI NATIONAL PARK.

If you don't fancy the long drive to Doi Inthanon National Park, Doi Suthep-Pui National Park is just a thirty-minute drive west of Chiang Mai. Doi Pui Mountain sits at 1,685 meters above sea level and is the highest peak in the Doi Suthep-Pui National Park. It is famous for its beautiful waterfalls, which are easily reached from the main road.

One of the main attractions in the Doi Pui area is the Hmong Tribal Village where you can visit the village and meet and chat with the Hmong to learn about their way of life.

LONG NECK KAREN TRIBAL VILLAGE.

The Karen are a tribal group who are originally from Myanmar who over the years fled to Thailand during the political unrest and persecution. Many of them now live in small villages one of which is in Mae Rim just outside of Chiang Mai. The visits to the villages are enlightening experiences as you get to see the tribal people going about their everyday lives whilst having to sell their products to tourists in order to feed themselves. It is the women who are most recognisable to tourists who come to Northern Thailand, as they are the ones who wear brass coils around their necks. Contrary to popular belief, the brass coils don't lengthen the neck but rather push down and deform the clavicle at the base of the neck. The Karen women commence wearing the coils at around 5 years of age and typically only take them off to change to a longer coil. Most of these tribal villages such as the Karen in northern Thailand make their money to live and support their families from tourists, as they do not have formal residency status in Thailand and are not legally permitted to work. Therefore, if visiting these villages, you will typically be asked to pay an admission fee and the villagers will also host markets where they offer for sale a range of traditional handmade goods such as bags, scarves and hats. The most popular location to see the Karen Long Neck Tribes in Chiang Mai is the Bann Tong Luang Village which is located just 25 kilometres north of Chiang Mai, or an approximate 30-minute drive from Chiang Mai city.

ROYAL PARK RATCHAPHRUEK.

Royal Park Ratchaphruek is a large botanical garden located at the Royal Agricultural Research Center and is a large public park and agricultural research centre with vast green areas, royal exhibitions, and different styles of gardens. The 240,000-square-metre park is divided into different zones such as the Thai Tropical Garden, the Orchid Garden where you can see colourful collections of rare orchids, and the International Gardens showcasing plants and landscaping designs from other countries. The park was opened in 2006 in honour of the then-king of Thailand, His Majesty King Bhumibol Adulyadej to celebrate the 60th Anniversary of His Majesty's Accession to the Throne and his 80th Birthday. A highlight of the park is the Ho Kham Luang Royal Pavilion, where an exhibit about the life and works of the late king is displayed.

SAN KAMPHAENG ROAD.

Also known as the *'Handicraft Highway'* San Kamphaeng Road is a long stretch of road where local artists practice their craft with a skill born of centuries-old traditions. Here you will find many shops and market stalls famous for their pottery, silverware, lacquerware, sculpting, and wood carvings but it is the Thai silk products that the area is mainly famous for. San Kamphaeng also has a bustling night Walking Street Market every Saturday night from 3:00 pm until

WHAT TO DO WHEN THE SUN GOES DOWN IN CHIANG MAI?
Chiang Mai has a vibrant nightlife as you would expect from such a busy tourist city. The city also has many bars and lady bars.

CHIANG MAI NIGHT MARKETS.
In the evening there are many night markets throughout the city. Most of them are in the more touristy areas like Old Town

THE NIGHT BAZAAR.
The Night Bazaar, Chiang Mai is directly east of the city moat, close to the Ping River on Chang Khlan Road. Chang Klan Road is just a normal street during the day, but at night the whole place lights up and becomes a booming night market when traders set up hundreds of market stalls along the road selling everything from fake designer gear to handcrafted goods as well as jewellery, toys, clothing, football shirts, carved elephants, artwork, sunglasses, shoes, luggage, furniture, homeware and CDs and DVDs You will also find handmade goods made by indigenous mountain tribes such as the Hmong and Karen Longneck. A lot of things will not have a price on so bartering is openly encouraged. When you're done with your shopping you will probably be in need of a cool drink so head to one of the dozens of nearby bars or restaurants to relax.

SUNDAY WALKING STREET MARKET.
Also known as the Sunday Market or the Walking Market this is probably the most famous of all the markets in Chiang Mai. This busy market opens every Sunday starting at Thapae Gate and runs along Rachadamnoen Road and Prapokkloa Road, but

it also spills over into many of the side streets. Many of the stalls sell handmade goods and as you walk through the market it is not uncommon to see the stall holders making their handicrafts in between selling their goods. As you walk through the market you will see several Buddhist temples and many food outlets selling Thai and Lanna specialities and local entertainers singing and performing traditional Thai, Hill Tribe or Lanna dances.

WUA LAI WALKING STREET.

The Chiang Mai Saturday Market or Wua Lai Market is located Southwest of the old city opposite the Chiang Mai Gate. The Market extends for roughly one kilometre down the length of Wua Lai Road when the road is closed mid-afternoon to all vehicular traffic and vendors set up their stalls. Many people prefer Saturday's Wua Lai Walking Street to the larger Sunday Market as it is not so busy but still has a large range of locally made products such as handicrafts, bags, clothing, perfume, shoes, belts, lanterns, silverware, wood carvings, arts and crafts, ornaments, candles and housewares. There are also street performers and many food stalls. The market is named after Wua Lai Road, which links to Thipanet Road, just off the south side of the old city walls.

WARROROT MARKET.

Warorot Market is one of the more local markets for locals in Chiang Mai. On the lower levels, you will find an array of fresh produce along with ready-to-eat snacks and meals. On the second and third levels, the stalls are dedicated to clothing and accessories. This market is more for locals but it's a great way to see how the Thai people live and maybe sample the ethnic food that they come to buy.

BARS AND NIGHTLIFE IN CHIANG MAI

With Chiang Mai being the second most visited tourist area in Thailand it does have an exciting nightlife scene and also has many lady bar areas scattered around the city. There are two kinds of bars in Chiang Mai. There are your regular bars and then there are your Lady Bars. For your regular bars, there are too many to choose from but the ones that stand out are worth checking out around the city.

SOME OF THE REGULAR BARS IN CHIANG MAI

CHILL OUT BAR.
Chill Out Bar is an outdoor bar renowned in Chiang Mai for its laid-back atmosphere and its great cocktails. The bar is just an outdoor street kiosk but it is very popular. Due to the small size of the bar, the tables fill up fast so get in early to ensure a seat. Located just inside the walled Old City the Chill Out Bar is conveniently placed for locals and tourists.

NORTH GATE JAZZ CO-OP.
If you like Jazz Music the North Gate Jazz Co-op is an intimate venue that plays host to a rotating line-up of the best local jazz musicians with the occasional jam sessions with visiting musicians. From time to time, they mix jazz with more pop-focused music to please the crowds. The venue sits right next to the North Gate of Chiang Mai's famous walled Old City.

THAPAE EAST BAR.
Thapae East is a small live music bar close to Chiang Mai's Narawat Bridge, just outside of the main tourist area of town. The bar operates as a cafe during the day, with the food continuing into the evening. The trendy bar hosts an eclectic mix of bands and musicians every evening from Jazz to funk to heavy rock to blues are just some of the diverse sounds you can expect at this venue depending on the musicians booked for that evening.

ZOE IN YELLOW.
Zoe In Yellow is a nightclub complex with pumping sounds and an exuberant party atmosphere. The nightclub features

multiple rooms playing a mix of commercial hip-hop and pulsating electronic rock music. The club is aimed at the young local set, tourists and local expats in search of a great night out. The drink menu includes beers, wine, spirits and cocktails. Zoe In Yellow is a great lively night out in Chiang Mai. You may also find some ladies who are freelancers in the club and are looking to find some paid-for company for the night.

WRITER'S CLUB & WINE BAR.

If you are looking for a more upmarket bar to hang out then look no further than the Writer's Club & Wine Bar. Known locally as the city's unofficial press club, the wine bar is a favourite haunt of local writers and media types due to its selection of good wine, its varied menu and its relaxed intimate atmosphere. Located inside Hotel California, it's a great option for those looking for a night out in a more discerning atmosphere without the crowds or the loud music.

BOY BLUES BAR.

The Boy Blues Bar hosts some of the best live music in Chiang Mai six nights a week. Headed by beloved owner and local musician, Boy, this trendy eclectic bar hosts bands playing a blend of blues and jazz, with Boy himself lighting up the stage alongside his talented house band on most evenings. The bar is above the Chiang Mai Night Bazaar, so you can enjoy a mixture of shopping, eating and drinking in this part of the city.

MINIMAL BAR.

Out of the old town of Chiang Mai in the Santitham area of town, you will find the trendy Minimal Bar. The owner of Minimal also owns the major independent record label in Chiang Mai "Minimal Records" and the club is one of the places where the hardcore music fans in Chiang Mai gather to talk about and listen to music. The bar is Minimal by name and nature, the stripped interior embodies the bar with a cosmopolitan feel. They offer a small food menu and the drink prices are reasonably priced

SOME OF THE LADY BARS IN CHIANG MAI

With Chiang Mai being a huge tourist destination there is no shortage of lady bars in the city many of them situated in the Old Town area of town.

LOI KROH ROAD.

Loi Kroh Road near the Ring Road intersection is the most well-known area for lady bars in the city. Here you will find many bars with beautiful ladies, and some not-so-beautiful, vying for your attention and offering to make you the happiest man in Chiang Mai for the night...for a price.

CHIANG MAI NIGHT BAZAAR.

Chiang Mai Night Bazaar is a quieter area of bars that sits just north of Loi Kroh Road and is located as the name suggests near the Night Bazaar.

THE FOOD IN CHIANG MAI

The food in Chiang Mai is out of this world. Most people I have spoken to who have lived in or visited Chiang Mai agree that it's probably one of the best places to eat in Thailand. You can smell that magnificent BBQ aroma everywhere you go when walking down the street that will always get my mouth watering. Chiang Mai also has their signature dishes that should not be missed, including Sai-ua which is spiced lemongrass sausages, Khao Soi is a delicious traditional northern Thailand noodle soup that is simply called Chiang Mai noodles, Gaeng Hunglay a northern Pork and Ginger Curry, and Laab Muanghai, spicy grilled pork. But be warned many of the local dishes are very spicey.

As for food markets, Warorot Market is probably the most well-known and is in the centre of the city's little Chinatown. The market is multistory shopping with many traditional shops; On the ground floor, you will find mostly food, with a selection of all the ingredients you need to cook authentic Thai food. Their fruit and vegetable stalls also offer a wide range of western fare as well as some of the weird and wonderful Thai fruit and vegetables. The other floors are mainly clothing, Thai and Chiang Mai artefacts. Ton Lamyai is another large market close to Warorot Market. As for shopping malls to buy food and other products there is an abundance in all areas of Chiang Mai including Maya Lifestyle Shopping Centre, Central Festival, Kad Suan Kaew Department Store, and Promenada Resort Mall. There are also two Big C Super Centres with an amazing display of Thai and Western foods.

CHIANG MAI'S HOSPITALS AND MEDICAL FACILITIES

If you are a retiree one of the most important aspects in your choice of where to live will be hospital and medical care. Medical care in Chiang Mai is second only to the capital, Bangkok, with many excellent private hospitals and medical facilities at reasonable prices.

Hospitals in Chiang Mai include:
Bangkok Hospital Chiang Mai
Sriphat Hospital

Lanna Hospital (Government Hospital)

Rajavej Hospital

Ram Hospital

Many of the top doctors in Chiang Mai have learned their profession in Western countries including Great Britain, the USA and many European countries. They are competent professionals and very caring towards their patients. Most of Chiang Mai's hospitals have websites where you can check out a doctor's credentials online, to help you choose the doctor you prefer before making an appointment. Many will speak fluent English and are accomplished specialist surgeons. Pharmacies are everywhere including Boots and Fascino Pharmacies. There are also many dental clinics to choose from scattered around the city.

THE DOWNSIDES OF LIVING IN CHIANG MAI.

Wherever you live in the world there are always going to be disadvantages as no town is 100% perfect. Some of the drawbacks of living in Chiang Mai are:

THE LONG DISTANCE FROM EVERYWHERE ELSE IN THAILAND:

Chiang Mai is a nine-hour drive to Bangkok and around a twelve-hour drive to the nearest beach. Koh Samui is a nineteen-hour drive plus a two-hour ferry crossing. Pattaya is an eleven-hour drive and Phuket is a twenty-one-hour drive so Chiang Mai may seem off the beaten track and if you are coming to live here with the idea of regular travel around Thailand then you may find that Chiang Mai is quite remote.

THE POLLUTION IN THE BURN OFF-SEASON:

Every year between January to March and sometimes longer

the area is infamously known because of *The Burn-Off Season*. This is a time when the air quality in the area is one of the worst in the world over that period. This is the time of the year when local farmers burn off their fields from the previous year's crops to prepare their land for the following year's crops and to rid the fields of biowastes. In Thailand, it's illegal to burn the fields as it causes harm to the environment and people's health but the government turn a blind eye to it and allows it to happen each year to appease the struggling farmers. The pollution can spike to AQI 300+ and is particularly bad for young children the elderly, and people with respiratory diseases, such as asthma, emphysema and bronchitis and they should avoid being outdoors during this period.

THE LANGUAGE BARRIER:
In the more touristy areas of the city, English is widely spoken but you may find that in the more remote parts of the city and the rural areas you will have difficulty with the language.

KOH SAMUI

CHAPTER TWO
KOH SAMUI

The island of Koh Samui is one of my favourite if not my very favourite place to live in Thailand. Since 2017 when I first arrived in Thailand to live, I have spent probably 50% of my time on the island and the beauty of the island never ceases to amaze me and is always calling me back. Koh Samui has a permanent population of over 70,000 people though that rises depending on the number of tourists arriving by air or ferries every day. In early 2020 when COVID arrived in the country it devastated the Thai economy. This impacted tourist areas such as Koh Samui and it ruined the island's thriving tourism industry for three years but from a selfish point of view when I was living there, I loved that there were hardly any foreign tourists clogging up the island and driving their rented motorbikes at crazy speeds and pushing up the prices in the bars and restaurants. Because there were hardly any foreign tourists over the Covid years, prices were low with the few restaurants, hotels, bars and associated businesses that managed to stay open dropping their prices to try to attract local expats and Thai tourists to the island. Because of this over the past few years, I have stayed in 3 or 4-star hotels directly on the beach and paid as little as 500 Baht a night whereas before covid arrived the same hotels would have been charging at least 2,000 Baht a night. As I am writing this it's January 2024 and the high season will soon be ending and the prices have gone back to their higher pre-covid rates over the high season. It remains to be seen what the prices will be in the off-season and the future but unless there's another worldwide health problem all indications are that the high season next year will be booming once again.

Koh Samui is known as the Coconut Island, due to the millions of tons of coconuts that were shipped from the island every year. When it comes to the ultimate beach lifestyle in Thailand, you can't go past Koh Samui which is part of Surat Thani Province. Koh Samui has golden beaches fantastic weather most of the year and clear blue seas. It's not all about the beach though. Look further afield and you will find crystal-clear waterfalls, Buddhist temples and verdant forests. It is an ideal destination for retirees on any budget. Just over an hour's flight from the Thai capital of Bangkok and about two hours by ferry from Donsak Pier, south of Surat Thani town. You can also get a ferry from Koh Samui to Koh Phangan and Koh Tao. There are three golf courses on the island

SOME FACTS ABOUT KOH SAMUI

- Population: The island of Koh Samui has a permanent population of over 70,000 though this goes up a lot with the many tourists that arrive on the island each year The island is known by the locals as just Samui, not Koh Samui, Koh in Thai means island.
- Temperature/Seasons: Koh Samui enjoys a tropical monsoon climate There are three distinct weather seasons in Koh Samui. The dry season (December until February), the hot season (March until August) and the rainy season (September until November).
- Koh Samui lies 754 kilometres south of Bangkok and 34km from Donsak Pier the main ferry port in Surat Thani on the Thai mainland. The island covers an area of 228 square kilometres and is 25 kilometres long x 21 kilometres wide and takes about an hour and a half to circumnavigate the island in a car or motorbike.
- Koh Samui is the second largest island in Thailand after Phuket.
- Koh Samui wasn't discovered by tourists until the early 1970s and didn't have any sealed roads until that time. Before that, the island was known for its fishing and coconut plantations.
- Koh Samui is in the Surat Thani Province and Nathon is the capital town of Koh Samui, while Chaweng is the entertainment heart of the island.
- The island is busy but it is not big enough to win the status of being its own province like Phuket has.
- Koh Samui is part of the Ang Thong Marine National Park which encompasses 80 mostly uninhabited islands.

THE WEATHER IN KOH SAMUI

May is the hottest month in Koh Samui with an average temperature of 30°C and the coldest is January at 26°C. The wettest month is November with an average of 430mm of rain. There are three seasons in Koh Samui, the dry season from December until February, the hot season from March until August and the rainy season from September until November.

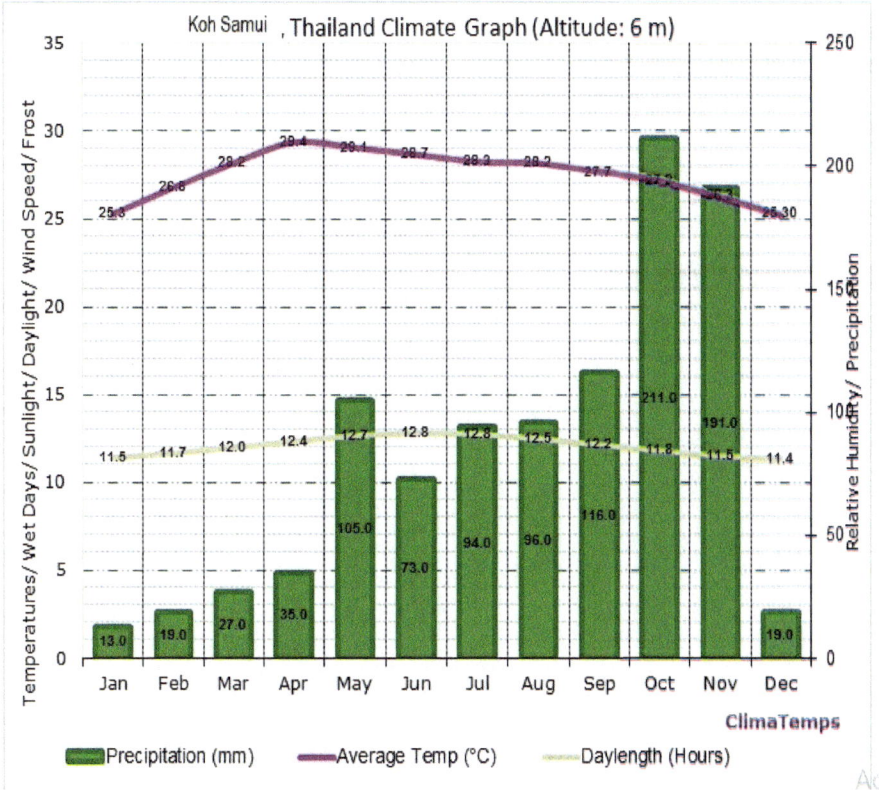

Koh Samui , Thailand Climate Graph (Altitude: 6 m)

Courtesy of www.travelfish.org

THE COST OF LIVING IN KOH SAMUI

The cost of living in Kho Samui is quite expensive compared to Chiang Mai. As on most Islands anywhere in the world you normally pay more for the privilege of living the island lifestyle than you do on the mainland. This is partly because of the extra costs involved in getting goods onto the island and partly because they can, you're on an island so they can charge what they want! But you're living the dream on a tropical Island so what the hell, right? Once again depends on your budget and the lifestyle you're looking for. As I said prices have risen since covid ended. A Studio condo will start at 1,500,000 Baht to buy. Condo rentals start at around 15,000 Baht a month for a one-bedroom, and 20,000 Baht for a two-bedroom but unless you sign a long-term lease those prices would probably rise in the high Season.

Rent Prices in Koh Samui are 14.2% lower than in Bangkok

Restaurant Prices in Koh Samui are 7.1% lower than in Bangkok

Groceries Prices in Koh Samui are 15.8% lower than in Bangkok

✗ Restaurants

Meal, Inexpensive Restaurant	100.00 ฿
Meal for 2 People, Mid-range Restaurant, Three-course	800.00 ฿
McMeal at McDonalds (or Equivalent Combo Meal)	250.00 ฿
Domestic Beer (0.5 liter draught)	70.00 ฿
Imported Beer (0.33 liter bottle)	95.00 ฿
Cappuccino (regular)	76.63 ฿
Coke/Pepsi (0.33 liter bottle)	25.61 ฿
Water (0.33 liter bottle)	15.36 ฿

🛒 Markets

Milk (regular), (1 liter)	53.54 ฿
Loaf of Fresh White Bread (500g)	46.50 ฿
Rice (white), (1kg)	23.33 ฿
Eggs (regular) (12)	73.89 ฿
Local Cheese (1kg)	602.00 ฿
Chicken Fillets (1kg)	85.75 ฿
Beef Round (1kg) (or Equivalent Back Leg Red Meat)	311.00 ฿
Apples (1kg)	110.57 ฿
Banana (1kg)	38.12 ฿
Oranges (1kg)	59.67 ฿
Tomato (1kg)	50.29 ฿
Potato (1kg)	44.12 ฿
Onion (1kg)	32.67 ฿
Lettuce (1 head)	30.00 ฿
Water (1.5 liter bottle)	14.00 ฿
Bottle of Wine (Mid-Range)	520.00 ฿
Domestic Beer (0.5 liter bottle)	57.32 ฿
Imported Beer (0.33 liter bottle)	81.57 ฿
Cigarettes 20 Pack (Marlboro)	140.00 ฿

🚌 Transportation

One-way Ticket (Local Transport)	50.00 ฿
Monthly Pass (Regular Price)	?
Taxi Start (Normal Tariff)	50.00 ฿
Taxi 1km (Normal Tariff)	50.00 ฿
Taxi 1hour Waiting (Normal Tariff)	450.00 ฿
Gasoline (1 liter)	41.79 ฿
Volkswagen Golf 1.4 90 KW Trendline (Or Equivalent New Car)	700,000.00 ฿
Toyota Corolla Sedan 1.6l 97kW Comfort (Or Equivalent New Car)	879,000.00 ฿

🏠 Utilities (Monthly)

Basic (Electricity, Heating, Cooling, Water, Garbage) for 85m2 Apartment	3,648.21 ฿
Mobile Phone Monthly Plan with Calls and 10GB+ Data	511.56 ฿
Internet (60 Mbps or More, Unlimited Data, Cable/ADSL)	506.58 ฿

🚲 Sports And Leisure

Fitness Club, Monthly Fee for 1 Adult	1,250.00 ฿
Tennis Court Rent (1 Hour on Weekend)	600.00 ฿
Cinema, International Release, 1 Seat	260.00 ฿

👶 Childcare

Preschool (or Kindergarten), Full Day, Private, Monthly for 1 Child	15,816.67 ฿
International Primary School, Yearly for 1 Child	290,000.00 ฿

👕 Clothing And Shoes

1 Pair of Jeans (Levis 501 Or Similar)	1,548.33 ฿
1 Summer Dress in a Chain Store (Zara, H&M, ...)	600.00 ฿
1 Pair of Nike Running Shoes (Mid-Range)	2,500.00 ฿
1 Pair of Men Leather Business Shoes	2,500.00 ฿

🛏 Rent Per Month

Apartment (1 bedroom) in City Centre	14,112.94 ฿
Apartment (1 bedroom) Outside of Centre	13,000.00 ฿
Apartment (3 bedrooms) in City Centre	42,500.00 ฿
Apartment (3 bedrooms) Outside of Centre	36,666.67 ฿

🏢 Buy Apartment Price

Price per Square Meter to Buy Apartment in City Centre	45,000.00 ฿
Price per Square Meter to Buy Apartment Outside of Centre	45,000.00 ฿

💳 Salaries And Financing

Average Monthly Net Salary (After Tax)	13,000.00 ฿
Mortgage Interest Rate in Percentages (%), Yearly, for 20 Years Fixed-Rate	3.82

Courtesy of www.numbeo.com

WHAT DOES KOH SAMUI OFFER FOR EXPATS LIVING THERE?

From my research, I have not been able to find a lot of expat clubs in Koh Samui. The only two I could find were the Hash House Harriers who proudly claim to be *"A Drinking Club with A*

Running Problem", and the women's only club Sisters of Samui, a group of international ladies who either live on Koh Samui or who are visiting, it's a charity but they also have social events. The main objective of the SOS is to meet, once a month, for lunch in convivial surroundings, enabling members to meet in friendship and to welcome any new arrivals. To become a member, there are no complex forms to complete or initiation ceremonies just turn up and introduce yourself. The only proviso is that you were "born a woman", I assume that means no ladyboys.

I think that Koh Samui is more for the fit and adventurous retiree, who loves the outdoor life and is still active. If you love the beach, swimming, diving, boating and great nightlife then this could be the place for you. Keep in mind the island always has an influx of tourists so things can get quite crowded, especially in the high season which also makes it a little more expensive.

***See Useful Website pages at the end of
this book for expat club links**

PLACES TO GO AND THINGS TO DO IN KOH SAMUI

POPULAR BEACHES OF KOH SAMUI

- **Chaweng Beach**
- **Lamai Beach**
- **Bophut Beach**
- **Choeng Mon**
- **Maenam Beach**
- **Lipa Noi Beach**

Being an island Samui has that tropical feel that many beach towns like Hua Hin, Pattaya and other Thai beach towns don't have and you are spoilt for choice as there are many secluded beaches on the island. Many tourists when they come to Samui just stick to the tourist beaches, but they miss out on seeing the real Samui by not going around the island to explore the bays and beaches that are mainly undiscovered by holidaymakers. Below are some of the popular beaches on Samui but there are so many more waiting for you to discover them.

Chaweng Beach

Chaweng Beach is Koh Samui's most popular beach and undoubtedly the most popular tourist area on Koh Samui though Lamai is not far behind in popularity. With its seven-kilometre beach, many water sports, shopping centres, bars and dining and entertainment venues, it is easy to see the attraction and why it's the tourist capital of the island. If you are hungry or thirsty you won't have to leave the beach as many vendors are walking along the beach selling a host of delicacies at reasonable prices, BBQ sweetcorn and chicken, fresh fruits, doughnuts, spicey papaya salad as well as ice cream and cold drinks. There are also massage huts along the beach as well as masseurs waking along the beach who will give you a massage where you are sitting. There are many hotels and restaurants lining the beach also.

Lamai Beach

Lamai Beach is Samui's second most popular beach and to me, it's a more beautiful beach than Chaweng. Not as touristy as Chaweng, Lamai Beach is a lot quieter and has a more laid-back feel to it. With its breathtaking crescent of palm-fringed white sand that stretches around the bay for about 5 kilometres, it's the perfect beach for spending a lazy day sunbathing, and swimming in the tranquil crystal-clear waters. You will find the same kind of vendors walking along the beach selling food drink and massage the same as you would in Chaweng in fact you will find the same kind of vendors on most tourist beaches in Thailand. You will also find many restaurants and bars all along the beach vying for your custom

Bophut Beach
Close to Samui's Big Buddha temple lies Bophut Beach. With its two kilometres of white sandy beach that's fringed by coconut palms, Bophut is an ideal place to chill out and relax and unwind and better still it is not as busy with tourists as Chaweng Beach and Lamai Beach are. If you are visiting Big Buddha or Wat Plai Laem you can take in this wonderful beach on the same day as they are close to each other.

Choeng Mon Beach
On the northwestern side of Samui lies Choeng Mon Beach is made up of a series of bays on the northwestern tip of the island. This area of Samui is hardly used by tourists so it's an ideal spot to escape the maddening crowds.

Maenam Beach
Maenam Beach is one of Samui's quietest beaches on the western side of the island. After spending some time swimming and relaxing on the wonderful tropical beach. As it's on the western side of the island if it's a cloudless evening you can watch the sunset over the horizon while sipping a cocktail in one of the many bars and restaurants along the beach or the coastal road.

Lipa Noi Beach
The uncrowded beach of Lipa Noi is largely ignored by the majority of tourists who come to Samui, which is a shame because it is one of the nicest beaches on the island. All along the beach, there are many cafes and restaurants. You can also find a few massage outlets where you can get a relaxing massage for just a couple of hundred baht. Lipa Noi Beach is my favourite place on the island to go for an amazing Koh Samui sunset.
There are many more secluded beaches all around the island

GERALDHOGG

such as Crystal Bay on the ring road between Lamai and Chaweng, Thongson Beach on the southeastern tip of the island and Nathon Beach which is on the western side of the island and a great place to go in the early evening to sip a cocktail and watch the sun go down.

As in all of Thailand temples play a big part in the daily lives of Buddhists in Samui. The great thing about Buddhism is that it is an inclusive religion and people of all faiths are welcome to enter their temples and they are greeted by the monks with a smile and a wai. There are many stunning temples to visit and they are usually strategically placed overlooking the Gulf of Thailand.

BIG BUDDHA
Samui has many temples the most famous being Big Buddha which is situated between Bophut and Choeng Mon. The 12-meter-long statue was built in 1972 and is located inside the temple grounds of Wat Phra Yai. It sits on a rocky island off Koh Samui's northeastern corner which is reached by a causeway that connects it to the main island. The Big Buddha sculpture sits in the Mara posture, with the upward-facing palm of the left hand resting on the lap and the right hand facing down. It depicts a time during Buddha's journey to enlightenment.

WAT PLAI LAEM
The Wat Plai Laem is probably my favourite temple on the island It is located in the northern part of the island and is, without question, one of the most beautiful temples in Samui if not the whole of Thailand, it sits on a lake that is filled with large fish and turtles. Just like the Big Buddha Temple, which is just a few minutes' drive down the road, Wat Plai Laem was built to impress, the temple's design incorporates elements

of Chinese, Indian and Thai traditions. The main statue is an eighteen-handed goddess of mercy, Guan Yin, who is said to help impoverished families' children grow happy and healthy, and she is also said to protect seamen from danger. Being an ex-seaman myself and knowing how dangerous working at sea can be, I appreciate her help. The other main statue is the happy Buddha who is known to give prosperity and happiness to those who pray to him.

WAT KHUNARAM (TEMPLE OF THE MUMMIFIED MONK)

Wat Khunaram is home to Koh Samui's mummified monk who sits in a glass display case within the temple and offers a unique insight into the Buddhist and Thai culture. The monk Luong Pordaeng who died in 1973 sits in a meditative position and remarkably almost 50 years after his death, the monk's body shows little sign of decay. For some foreign visitors who come here, having a dead man in full view might be a shocking sight. But for Thais, it's something to reflect upon and honour, as far from being afraid of death, most Buddhists accept death and the end of life as being the natural order of things and they view death as an opportunity to be reborn into a better place and a better life and one step closer to nirvana. The temple is just a ten-minute drive from Lamai on the island ring road.

LAEM SOR PAGODA

This chedi is situated at Laem Sor and is one of the most important shrines on Koh Samui. The temple is in Bang Kao on the South West corner of the island and sits proudly overlooking the Gulf of Thailand with its yellow tiles it gives off a golden aura in the sunlight and is well worth the drive to take in not just the temple but the stunning scenery of Bang Kao.

KHAO HUA JOOK PAGODA TEMPLE

With 360° panoramic views of Koh Samui and an incredible view of the airport, Khao Hua Jook Pagoda Temple in Chaweng near the lake is a beautiful temple but the stunning views are what brings many people here as the temple offers some of the finest views across the island.

SECRET BUDDHA GARDEN

Secret Buddha Garden also known as Tarnim Magic Garden is

a private sculpture park sitting on top of Pom Mountain which is one of the highest peaks on the island. The site looks like a temple but it is a private undertaking by a retired durian farmer, Khun Nim Thongsuk, who began building it in 1976, at the age of 77, and continued to do so until his death at the age of 91. The site features many statues of Buddha and other aspects of Thai Buddhism, and also of birds snakes and other animals, and a pair of statues of the founder's parents and a statue depicting him and his father. The main group of statues on the site are a number of angel statues and a group of musicians. Khun Nim's tomb is also found on the site, up a short path from the angel statues. The site also features many mossy waterfalls within the garden.

JUNGLE CLUB VIEWPOINT
Samui has some fantastic lookouts and viewpoints but The Jungle Club Viewpoint is my favourite place on the island to take in the beautiful vistas of Samui. While taking in the stunning view you can relax on one of the Jungle Club's bean bags and have a drink or have lunch on the deck or in their restaurant. The views stretch to the tip of Lamai around Chaweng and beyond.

LAD KOH VIEWPOINT
Lad Koh Viewpoint is one of the best places in Koh Samui where you can see spectacular panoramic views of the ocean from Chaweng to Lamai. The viewpoint is located between Lamai and Chaweng Beach on the main ring road that goes around the island., visitors can walk down along the paved path to the rugged coastline. If you're an early riser the viewpoint is a great place to watch the sunrise over the island.

LAMAI VIEWPOINT
Lamai Viewpoint is located on Mount Laem Mai and is surrounded by tropical jungle overlooking Lamai Beach. You Won't have to worry about trekking up the mountain on foot

there is a cable car that takes you to the top of the mountain where you can take in the views and sit and have a cold drink or lunch.

FISHERMAN'S VILLAGE

Fisherman's Village in Bophut is a thriving fishing community, and a popular walking street, with rustic shophouses converted into restaurants, food and drink outlets, shops and beach bars. Many of the restaurants here specialise in freshly caught local seafood, with both Thai and international cuisine. There's also a thriving night market on Friday nights.

GRANDFATHER AND GRANDMOTHER ROCK (HIN TA HIN YAI)

Grandfather and Grandmother Rock. on the southern end of Lamai Beach are one of the most popular attractions on Samui and they are a source of amusement for tourists The reason why they are so famous is the rock formations resemble male and female genitalia. There are some great beach bars and restaurants here also and there are some market stalls selling phallic souvenirs.

SHOPPING

If you need to do some shopping there are two huge shopping centres in Chaweng. Central Festival is in the middle of town and Tesco Lotus Shopping Centre is a little way out of town on the main ring road. There are also large Tesco Lotus shopping centres in Lamai and Nathon.

SAMUI AQUARIUM AND TIGER ZOO.

The undersea world of the aquarium has an amazing collection of tropical fish, sharks, octopuses, sea lions turtles and other aquatic sea life. The tiger zoo is home to Bengal tigers and leopards where you can have your photograph taken with these wild animals.

There are many other things to see and do on Samui depending on what you like to do with your time. With the wonders of the internet, it's easy to do a Google search of anything that you would like to do while you're in Thailand and see what comes up.

WHAT TO DO WHEN THE SUN GOES DOWN ON KOH SAMUI

The majority of tourists who come to Samui stay in Chaweng or Lamai during their stay on the island because those towns are the centre for most things that happen on the island. In these towns, you will witness some magnificent sunrises because they are on the eastern side of the island. But if you want to see a magnificent sunset while sipping a cocktail before dining on the beach you will need to go to the western side of the island to somewhere like Lipa Noi, Nathon or Tailing Ngam. Along the beach road at Nathon, you will find many great restaurants and bars with outside decking over the water where you can have a drink or dine while watching the sun go down over the horizon. Other places to go are The Chill Inn and The Nikki Beach Resort in Lipa Noi or I-Talay Beach Bar in Tailing Ngam

For nightlife, the two main places to kick up your heels are Chaweng and Lamai. Here is where you will find many of the lady bars that Koh Samui and Thailand are famous for.

CHAWENG

SOI GREEN MANGO

Koh Samui's most famous lady bar area and entertainment strip is Soi Green Mango in the heart of Chaweng. It's a circular alley just off the main road that meanders through town and it is close to The ARKbar. The most popular place on Soi Green Mango is Henry Africa's Bar but there are many others to choose from there are also three nightclubs in the complex and a few massage shops.

SOI REGGAE

Soi Reggae is a kilometre-long street of lady bars that is situated just behind Chaweng Lake. The name derives from the popular Reggae Pub at the end of the soi which is one of the oldest music and bar venues in Samui. Since COVID arrived and then left leaving broken businesses in its wake, Soi Reggae had been in decline with many bars closing and others up for sale, but recently the area seems to be improving with tourism being on the rise again.

THE ARKbar

The ARKbar Beach Club is famous on the island as the one-stop party destination and sits in the heart of Chaweng's downtown beach area. It is not just a bar but an all-day beach club that opens for breakfast and continues until the early hours of the morning seven days a week. This massive bar also has two stunning restaurants with a selection of food that caters to all tastes including a range of local Thai dishes with spicy and non-spicy options and western fare.

CHAWENG NIGHT MARKET

Chaweng Night Market runs along the length of Chaweng Lake. The market is packed with food stalls offering a great selection of dining options including many Thai outlets, as well as European and other Asian choices.

LAMAI

WALKING STREET

On Lamai's Walking Street, opposite Mcdonald's, you will find a huge lady bar area with about twenty bars and many ladies touting for your custom. In the centre of the bar area is a Muay Thai boxing ring that on some evenings has Thai lady kick boxers enter the ring to entertain their many customers.

SOI HAD LAMAI 1 AND SAMUI MOON SOI

Soi Had Lamai 1 and Samui Moon Soi are the other two main bar areas in Lamai. Not all bars in Chaweng and Lamai are lady bars there are also your normal bars that just sell food and drink but don't sell ladies. In the main towns and the more touristy areas on the island, you will find that wherever Western tourists frequent they will cater for every food taste imaginable from most people's home countries and many of those bars have live sports from many different countries to try to attract your business. Lamai used to have probably the best night market in Koh Samui that was open every Friday and Saturday night until COVID-19 arrived and ruined the tourist industry. Unfortunately, it never re-opened but hopefully one day it will open again as it is sorely missed.

LAMAI COCKTAILS

Lamai Cocktails used to be the famous Cocktail by Piks which was a favourite with many tourists and expats for many years due to its fantastic selection of good cheap cocktails. It was recently purchased by a European man and I thought that perhaps he would change everything and that the prices would go up and it would lose the unique atmosphere that it had as Cocktails by Pik, but when I last visited, I was pleasantly surprised. The cocktails were as good as ever the atmosphere was just the same and if anything, the bar was run more professionally with the staff being more attentive and happier. Where else can you get quality cocktails at happy hour from 3.00 pm until 6.00 pm for 75 baht and the rest of the evening for 90 baht?

GASTRO LAE LAY

This restaurant is hidden behind Café Amazon and sits right on the beach about a seven-minute drive from the centre of Lamai going south on the island ring road, close to the Muslim Village. It's a beautiful outdoor bar and restaurant and being out of town it doesn't attract too many tourists which is a blessing but the atmosphere and food are fantastic. Some nights they have live music and some nights they have a fire show and traditional Thai dancers.

BOPHUT

FISHERMAN'S VILLAGE AND FRIDAY NIGHT MARKET

Fisherman's Village is located on the North Coast in Bophut. On Walking Street, running parallel to the beach. The market is open every Friday from 5.00 pm to 11.00 pm. It's not just a night market there are plenty of bars, souvenir shops, massage parlours, and restaurants along the strip.

THE FOOD IN KOH SAMUI

Over the past few years because of the COVID-19 pandemic, a lot of restaurants, market stalls and food outlets have had to close due to lack of customers but this season has seen many of them reopen. Sadly, some of them have been unable to re-open due to the buildings falling into disrepair due to lack of maintenance since COVID started and tourism declined. But this high season the place was buzzing and had got its mojo back, which was great to see.

Unlike Chiang Mai Koh Samui does not have its own regional dishes. You will find all the spicey curries, stir fry's, noodles and rice dishes that you find elsewhere in Thailand. It does however have several world-class restaurants featuring extremely talented chefs. Being an island, the menus often feature a stunning selection of fresh seafood locally caught that day. For the less well healed there are many local food markets as well as food stalls scattered around the island selling cheap Thai food and drinks. Being one of the main foreign tourist destinations in Thailand there is no shortage of restaurants serving cuisine from most Western countries including USA Burger and rib joints, German, Italian, English, Australian, Swiss and even the Caribbean the list goes on.

KOH SAMUI HOSPITALS AND MEDICAL FACILITIES

Considering Koh Samui is just a small island 25 kilometres long x 21 kilometres wide, it has some of the best hospitals in Thailand. Normally retirees who want to retire to a tropical island have to consider how to get off the island in the event of a medical emergency. This quite often involves a medical flight from the island and unless you have top medical cover that could cost you a small fortune. In Koh Samui, you don't have to worry about that, as the hospitals are as good as anywhere in Thailand

Hospitals in Koh Samui include:

Bandon International Private Hospital

Bangkok Hospital Samui

Samui International Hospital

Thai International Hospital

Many of the doctors in these hospitals will have attended university or medical school in the West and are highly skilled; they will almost certainly be able to speak English.

THE DOWNSIDES OF LIVING IN KOH SAMUI

EXPENSIVE TO GET ON OR OFF THE ISLAND WHEN FLYING

It's very expensive to fly in and out of Koh Samui because Koh Samui Airport is owned by Bangkok Airways and they have a monopoly on the incoming and outgoing flights with mainly Bangkok Airways flights flying to and from the island. To get to Koh Samui it's much cheaper to fly to Surat Thani Airport on the mainland and then take a bus from there to Donsak Pier then get the ferry to the island. It will take you about 5-hours more to do it this way because Surat Thani Airport is about a three-hour bus ride away and then a 2-hour ferry crossing to Koh Samui. But for me, it's worth it for the money that I save.

A LONG WAY FROM MANY OTHER PLACES IN THAILAND
With an area of 514.000 square kilometres, Thailand is a massive country to get around. The distance from the Laos border in the north to the Malaysian border in the south is 1650 kilometres and from east to west and is 780 kilometres at its widest point. Koh Samui is a long way from many of the towns that you may one day like to visit. Bangkok is 800 kilometres, Chiang Mai is 1,500 kilometres, Pattaya is 900 kilometres, Udon Thani is 1,350 kilometres and Khon Kaen is a 1,200-kilometre drive. On the plus side, Krabi and Phuket are within a fairly short driving distance and the Malaysian border at Perlis is just 390 kilometres away.

ISLAND LIVING
Koh Samui has an area of 228 square kilometres and is 21 kilometres wide and 25 kilometres long so it's not a massive island. Though island living may suit many people it might not suit everyone as living on an island can sometimes feel quite claustrophobic and restrictive once you have got over the novelty of living on a secluded island. You can't just hop in your car or on your motorbike and leave the island whenever the mood takes you as you would need to take a ferry to the mainland and they don't run 24 hours a day. Also being an island, most things have to be flown, driven or shipped to the island and this incurs expenses that will have to be passed on to

the consumer, so many things are more expensive than on the mainland.

TO MANY TOURISTS

Rated as one of the most beautiful islands in the world, Koh Samui can sometimes be overcrowded with tourists, especially during the high season between late November and February, which also coincides with the dry season. During this time, the island is at its busiest, with many tourists coming to enjoy the warm weather and beautiful beaches and the roads are crowded with hordes of tourists who have hired motorbikes and cars. Many tourists in Koh Samui also mean higher prices unless you shop and eat where the locals shop and eat.

BANGKOK

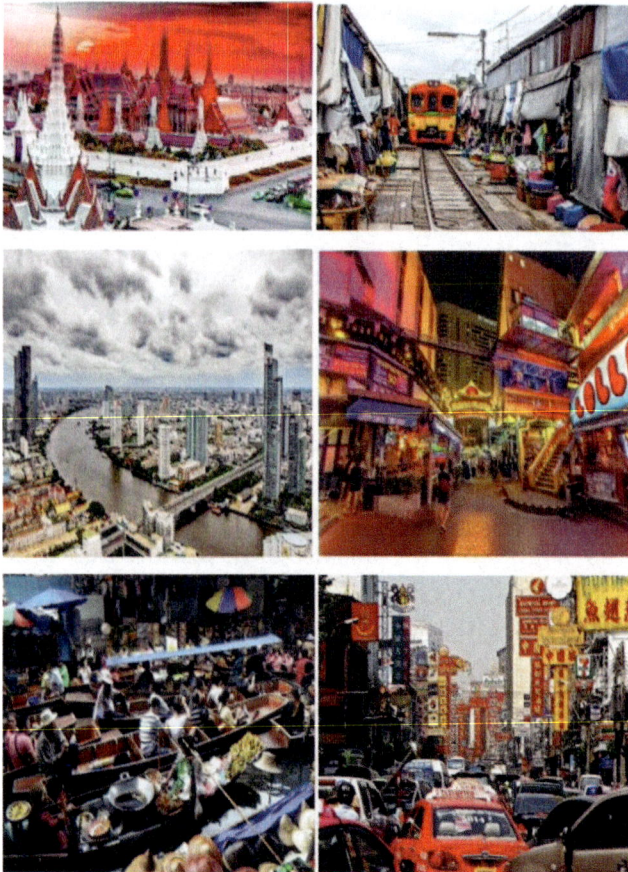

CHAPTER THREE

BANGKOK

Bangkok is a city of over ten million people, with a fair few of them being expats and retirees. It is a city of contrasts, that manages to blend the old with the new which makes the city exciting and eclectic.

As in any capital city in the world, Bangkok offers many attractions and entertainment venues as well as many shopping centres, markets and sporting events. The city has a rich cultural heritage with countless museums and galleries, temples and many festivals, with Songkran and Loi Krathong being the most famous. The Grand Palace sits in the heart of Bangkok along the banks of the Chao Phraya River and is the residence of King Maha Vajiralongkorn, the palace has been the official residence of the Kings of Siam, later to be called Thailand, since 1782.

There are more markets in Bangkok than anywhere else in Thailand and perhaps Southeast Asia. Here you will find night markets, train markets, fresh food markets, farmers' markets and weekend markets all of which go hand in hand with living in Bangkok. The transport and infrastructure in Bangkok are as good as any city in the world and the MRT underground is fantastic, with routes to all of the major areas of Bangkok. With their two airports, Don Mueang and Suvarnabhumi Airport, travelling to other countries or anywhere within Thailand is convenient and easy. Bangkok also has a magnificent train service that runs the length and breadth of the country as well as bus and coach services that service the surrounding areas and the whole of the country.

The nightlife in Bangkok is well known throughout the world, such as the lady bar scene in areas like Nana Plaza and Soi Cowboy but they also have a more sophisticated nightlife scene throughout the city.

If you have never lived in a large city before, I would recommend that you come and spend at least a few months here to see how you adapt, before making any big decisions. If golf is your thing there are more than forty golf courses scattered around Bangkok and the surrounding areas.

FACTS ABOUT BANGKOK

- Population: The city of Bangkok has a population of over eleven million. This makes it the second largest city in Southeast Asia by population, after Jakarta in Indonesia. The Greater Bangkok area has a population of over fourteen million, this includes five provinces that surround the city: Pathum Thani, Samut Prakan, Samut Sakhon, Nakhom Pathom, and Nonthaburi. Every day, an additional one million people enter Bangkok City from the suburbs for work. Bangkok is the 33rd largest city in the world by population with ten per cent of the population of Thailand living in the Bangkok area.

- Temperature/Seasons: Bangkok enjoys a tropical monsoon climate with three main seasons: a hot season from March to June, a rainy season from July to October, and a cool season between November and February. In one of the hottest cities in the world, expect daytime temperatures to be over 30°C for most of the year. enjoys a tropical monsoon climate with three main seasons:

- Bangkok's Chinatown is said to be the largest Chinatown in the world. Known locally as Yaowarat, Chinatown is home to over a million ethnic Chinese. In the daytime, shops and stalls sell products at some of the cheapest prices in the city and at night the area is transformed into a street food market, with hundreds of vendors selling every kind of Chinese, Asian or Thai food imaginable. Chinatown also boasts the largest solid gold Buddha in the world, inside Wat Traimit. The five-and-a-half-ton Buddha was hidden inside plaster for hundreds of years and it was only discovered that it was solid gold when it was accidentally dropped while moving

it
- Chatuchak Weekend Market is claimed to be the largest market in the world with around 8,000 stalls.
- Although the capital city of Thailand is known as Bangkok, local people refer to it as Krung Thep. which is a shortened version of the actual name, The full name is Krungthepmahanakhon Amonrattanakosin Mahinthara Yutthaya Mahadilok Phop Noppharat Ratchathani Burirom Udom Ratchaniwet Mahasathan Amonphiman Awatansathit Sakkathattiya Witsanukamprasit. Which translates to City of Angels, the great city of immortals, magnificent city of the nine gems, the seat of the king, city of royal palaces, home of gods incarnates, erected by Visvakarman at Indra's behest.
- All the temples stamped on the back of Thai coins are in Bangkok:

1-Baht coin – Wat Phra Kaew (Temple of the Emerald Buddha, inside The Grand Palace)

2-Baht coin – Wat Saket (Temple on the Mount)

5-Baht coin – Wat Benjamabophit (The Marble Temple)

10-Baht coin – Wat Arun (Temple of Dawn)

- Bangkok wasn't the original capital of Thailand. The city of Ayutthaya was founded in 1350 and became the capital of the Siamese Kingdom (now Thailand). The historical city flourished and became one of the world's largest diverse urban areas with a growing economy. The city was strategically surrounded by three rivers and is situated above the tidal bore of the Siam Gulf, preventing attacks from other nations, and protecting the city from seasonal flooding. However, in 1767, the Burmese army attacked Ayutthaya City, leaving it burnt to the ground and forcing its residents to flee and abandon the city. Ayutthaya is now an archaeological site as it was never rebuilt and the capital was later situated in Bangkok.

THE WEATHER IN BANGKOK

The weather in Bangkok is dominated by a tropical monsoon climate which means there are three main seasons: the hot season from March to June, the rainy season from July to October and the cool season between November and February. Because of the smog caused by so much traffic, the humidity is also very high in the city.

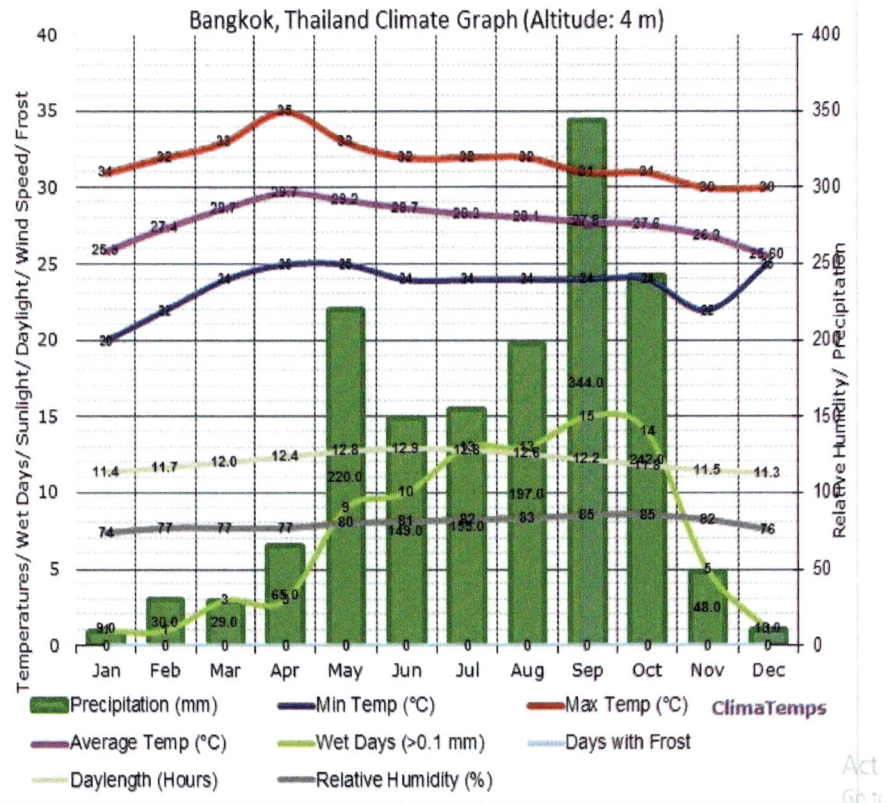

Bangkok, Thailand Climate Graph (Altitude: 4 m)

Courtesy of www.travelfish.org

THE COST OF LIVING IN BANGKOK

Like most capital cities around the world, Bangkok is more expensive to live in than other places in Thailand though Phuket and Pattaya are comparable. The cost of living in Bangkok will depend on your lifestyle. It can be one of the most affordable cities or one of the most expensive as the city caters to the very rich as well as the middle class and the poor. Lifestyle preferences will vary from person to person but Bangkok is a city that seems to appeal to people from all walks of life, with many opportunities for a great lifestyle at a very low price compared to most Western country's capital cities. Condo rentals start at about 15,000 Baht for a basic small condo in the outer city areas. For 20,000 to 30,000 Baht, you can get a very nice one or two-bedroom condo within the city. To buy a condo in Bangkok the price starts at about 3 million Baht for a small unit to 40 million Baht and above for an spectacular upmarket unit. It may cost you a little more to eat out here than in most other places in Thailand but not excessively so unless you go to the upmarket restaurants, on the flip side the city is teaming with markets, food stalls and cheap eateries.

✗ Restaurants

Meal, Inexpensive Restaurant	100.00 ฿
Meal for 2 People, Mid-range Restaurant, Three-course	1,000.00 ฿
McMeal at McDonalds (or Equivalent Combo Meal)	200.00 ฿
Domestic Beer (0.5 liter draught)	80.00 ฿
Imported Beer (0.33 liter bottle)	122.50 ฿
Cappuccino (regular)	82.74 ฿
Coke/Pepsi (0.33 liter bottle)	20.95 ฿
Water (0.33 liter bottle)	12.07 ฿

🛒 Markets

Milk (regular), (1 liter)	60.97 ฿
Loaf of Fresh White Bread (500g)	54.32 ฿
Rice (white), (1kg)	51.35 ฿
Eggs (regular) (12)	74.51 ฿
Local Cheese (1kg)	695.47 ฿
Chicken Fillets (1kg)	109.11 ฿
Beef Round (1kg) (or Equivalent Back Leg Red Meat)	393.60 ฿
Apples (1kg)	107.05 ฿
Banana (1kg)	47.07 ฿
Oranges (1kg)	78.76 ฿
Tomato (1kg)	56.36 ฿
Potato (1kg)	54.91 ฿
Onion (1kg)	47.17 ฿
Lettuce (1 head)	44.98 ฿
Water (1.5 liter bottle)	15.49 ฿
Bottle of Wine (Mid-Range)	700.00 ฿
Domestic Beer (0.5 liter bottle)	59.82 ฿
Imported Beer (0.33 liter bottle)	109.98 ฿
Cigarettes 20 Pack (Marlboro)	150.00 ฿

🚗 Transportation

One-way Ticket (Local Transport)	44.00 ฿
Monthly Pass (Regular Price)	1,300.00 ฿
Taxi Start (Normal Tariff)	35.00 ฿
Taxi 1km (Normal Tariff)	40.00 ฿
Taxi 1hour Waiting (Normal Tariff)	180.00 ฿
Gasoline (1 liter)	39.83 ฿
Volkswagen Golf 1.4 90 KW Trendline (Or Equivalent New Car)	1,950,000.00 ฿
Toyota Corolla Sedan 1.6l 97kW Comfort (Or Equivalent New Car)	910,309.52 ฿

🛁 Utilities (Monthly)

Basic (Electricity, Heating, Cooling, Water, Garbage) for 85m2 Apartment	3,228.71 ฿
Mobile Phone Monthly Plan with Calls and 10GB+ Data	467.87 ฿
Internet (60 Mbps or More, Unlimited Data, Cable/ADSL)	561.37 ฿

🚴 Sports And Leisure

Fitness Club, Monthly Fee for 1 Adult	2,061.06 ฿
Tennis Court Rent (1 Hour on Weekend)	376.71 ฿
Cinema, International Release, 1 Seat	270.00 ฿

🛵 Childcare

Preschool (or Kindergarten), Full Day, Private, Monthly for 1 Child	22,673.32 ฿
International Primary School, Yearly for 1 Child	466,561.36 ฿

👕 Clothing And Shoes

1 Pair of Jeans (Levis 501 Or Similar)	1,951.46 ฿
1 Summer Dress in a Chain Store (Zara, H&M, ...)	1,469.02 ฿
1 Pair of Nike Running Shoes (Mid-Range)	3,478.28 ฿
1 Pair of Men Leather Business Shoes	3,363.96 ฿

🛏 Rent Per Month

Apartment (1 bedroom) in City Centre	24,851.85 ฿
Apartment (1 bedroom) Outside of Centre	11,719.44 ฿
Apartment (3 bedrooms) in City Centre	58,162.76 ฿
Apartment (3 bedrooms) Outside of Centre	29,246.77 ฿

🏢 Buy Apartment Price

Price per Square Meter to Buy Apartment in City Centre	195,615.38 ฿
Price per Square Meter to Buy Apartment Outside of Centre	89,471.63 ฿

Courtesy of www.numbeo.com

WHAT DOES BANGKOK OFFER FOR EXPATS LIVING THERE?

What many expats in Thailand love about living in Bangkok is the unique blend of Asian and Western cultures. It also offers a cheaper quality of life than back home in your own country.

With over half a million expats from many countries around the world reported to be living in Bangkok and many more visiting the city every year from around Thailand and around the world, it won't be too hard to find people from your home country or even your home town. There is also the usual collection of Irish, British, Australian, USA and European bars should you want to catch up on sport or politics or have a meal like your mum used to cook. Most of the bars have live coverage of sports from their own countries, such as soccer from the UK, American football from the USA, and Aussie rules from Australia. You can eat roast beef and Yorkshire pud in many UK bars on a Sunday and Fish N Chips on a Friday, Buffalo wings and cheeseburgers in the USA bars and Australian meat pies in their bars while drinking a beer from your motherland. You can even read a recent newspaper from home while you're eating, there are also several expat clubs. The Bangkok Expats Meetup Club is popular. There is even a Lions Club in the city. Probably the most famous ex-pat club is the very colonial-looking The British Club. The club has been in business for over one hundred years on the same premises, so they must be doing something right. The club is the social, sports & cultural centre for the English-speaking community in Bangkok but they have a large membership from over 40 countries. The Club has a wide range of sporting and social activities for the whole family.

***See Useful Website pages at the end of
this book for expat club links**

PLACES TO GO AND THINGS TO DO IN BANGKOK

Bangkok is one of the most vibrant cities in all of Asia if not the world. The Thai capital is a city of contrasts where old meets new. A city where you can eat unpretentious street food at a market stall for just a few baht or wine and dine at a ritzy upmarket rooftop restaurant and pay high prices that you may pay in comparable restaurants in London, New York, Rome or

GERALDHOGG

Paris. A city where you can travel in air-conditioned comfort in a rented limousine or get around the city on the modern metro and elevated Skytrain or take a Tuk-Tuk, motorbike taxi or a Songthaew around the city to take in all the sights that the city has to offer. Or if the mood takes you, you can take a traditional longtail boat ride down the Chao Phraya River throughout Bangkok's network of canals.

There are some fantastic green areas in Bangkok, Benjakitti Park is a 480,000-square-meter public park and green space which is almost as big as London's Hyde Park and sits in the Khlong area in the centre of Bangkok. A little further up the road sits an even bigger park, Lumphini Park a 574,000 square meter green space, both parks offer rare open public spaces and Lumphini Park is regarded as the first public park in Bangkok and Thailand. Both parks are relaxing places to escape the busy city area and a great way to start your day. There are so many places to see and so many things to do in Bangkok that you will never get bored, so, the places below are the most popular places to visit.

THE GRAND PALACE

The first place many tourists want to see when visiting Bangkok and the most visited site in the whole of Thailand is The Grand Palace. The Grand Palace sits on the Phraya River in the heart of Bangkok, spans 218,000 square meters and features temples, stupas, government offices, throne halls, a Buddhist library, and beautifully manicured gardens. As with London's Buckingham Palace, Thailand's Grand Palace is the most visited attraction in Bangkok by foreign tourists. There is strict security so before you can enter the Grand Palace you will need to go through a bag search and produce your ID. Thailand being Thailand sometimes lets people in without having to show ID but it's better to be safe than sorry and carry some ID with you at all times wherever you are in Thailand such as a valid driver's license also, Thailand is very strict on dress codes for entering temples and Thai places of reverence so it's best to dress appropriately to ensure that you are not turned away when visiting any places of significance.

WAT PHO

Sitting next to the Grand Palace is Wat Pho or as it is more commonly known, the temple of Reclining Buddha. The temple is top of the list of six temples in Thailand that are classed as the highest grade of the first-class royal temples. This stunning temple has over a thousand Buddha images and is reputed to be the largest collection of Buddha images in Thailand, but the main attraction in the wat is the golden Reclining Buddha, which is 46 meters long and 15 meters high and takes up the entire temple and is a magnificent work of art.

WAT ARUN (THE TEMPLE OF DAWN)

Just a short boat ride across the Phraya River from Wat Pho sits another temple that as you are in the area you should not miss. With more than 37,000 temples throughout Thailand, Wat Arun is one of the most acclaimed. The 269-foot-tall Khmer-style tower sits high above the banks of the Chao Phraya River. The highlight of this temple is a 79-metre-tall central pagoda, "Phra Prang", and four smaller ones at each corner. The ornamentation of the central pagoda consists of encrusted pieces of porcelain which sparkle in the sun. In the evening the entire temple is illuminated in a golden glow, so it may also be worth your while coming in the evening to see the temple in its full glory. The temple derives its name from the Hindu god Aruna and is personified by the radiations of the rising sun. To visit the temple, shuttle boats from the Tha Tian Pier at the southwestern side of the Grand Palace and Wat Phra Kaeo area depart regularly. If like me you love visiting Buddhist temples there are many more stunning temples to see in Bangkok such as Wat Benchamabophit (The Marble Temple), Wat Saket (The Golden Mount), Wat Ratchabophit, Wat Suthat, and Wat Indhara Wihan...the list goes on.

CHATUCHAK MARKET

Chatuchak Weekend Market in Bangkok is locally known as

JJ Market and was once only popular among wholesalers and traders, but it is now on the tourist map as a must-visit place for residents and visitors to the Thai capital. If it's the weekend, Chatuchak Market is a great place to spend a few hours. Chatuchak is home to more than 8,000 market stalls that are spread over more than 14 hectares and the sheer size of the Chatuchak market is part of what makes it such a popular destination in Bangkok. You can find just about anything at Chatuchak Market, clothing & accessories, handicrafts, ceramics, pets and pet accessories, furniture and home decoration, books, antiques, art and of course food from many countries. The Market is located near the Bangkok Bus Terminal (Mo Chit II).

JIM THOMPSON'S HOUSE MUSEUM

Jim Thompson was an American entrepreneur who came to Thailand after serving in Southeast Asia during the 2nd World War and he devoted his life to developing the Thai silk industry. Jim Thompson disappeared mysteriously from Malaysia's Cameron Highlands in 1967 and his disappearance from the hill station generated one of the largest land searches in Southeast Asian history and still remains to this day one of the most famous mysteries in the region. After his assumed tragic death, the house was preserved as a museum containing priceless collections of Asian objects d'art.

AYUTTHAYA

Thailand's former capital, Ayutthaya is the most popular of all the day trips from Bangkok. This UNESCO World Heritage Site sits on a sprawling 289 hectares and was once the capital of Siam. and is renowned for its temple ruins. On arrival at Ayutthaya, most visitors head first to the Ayutthaya Historical Park and looking at the ruins, it's easy to imagine the grandeur that once was the kingdom of Ayutthaya. The complex has many old temples including Wat Phra Si Sanphet, Wat Yai Chai Mongkol and its 121-foot-long reclining Buddha statue, and Wat

Mahathat which is very much like Cambodia's iconic Angkor Wat. Most of the temples in Ayutthaya are open from 8.00 am until 5.00 pm. You can purchase a package ticket, including six temples, for 220 baht.

There are many more things to see and do in Bangkok depending on your requirements and how you like to spend your leisure time and with Bangkok being the capital city the list is endless.

WHAT TO DO WHEN THE SUN GOES DOWN IN BANGKOK?

CHAO PHRAYA RIVER DINNER CRUISE

Along the banks of the Chao Phraya River close to the Grand Palace you will find many boats offering unforgettable River Dinner Cruises. The Chao Phraya River is the heartbeat of Bangkok and is what gave Bangkok its name, "The Venice of the East" so taking a boat tour along the river is an attraction in itself. But taking a dinner cruise down the river in an antique wooden rice barge while enjoying a six-course dinner and seeing the Grand Palace and Wat Arun illuminated as a backdrop is a great way to end a day in Bangkok.

KHAO SAN ROAD

Khao San Road is famous around the world with travellers and you may think that it's a massive thoroughfare but in real life, it is just a short 400-meter soi. It was constructed in 1892 during the reign of Rama V and lies about one kilometre north of the Grand Palace and Wat Phra Kaew. Khao San translates as "milled rice", which as the name suggests in former times the street was a major rice market. Since tourism arrived in Thailand in the early 1970s with mainly backpackers at that time Khaosan Road has developed into a world-famous backpacker destination and it offers cheap accommodation, ranging from shared bunk room accommodation to reasonably priced two or three-star hotels. At night the shops on Khao San Road open up to sell handicrafts, paintings, clothes, local fruits, pirate CDs and DVDs, a wide range of fake IDs, used books, and other useful backpacker items. After dark, bars open, music is played, and food hawkers sell barbecued insects and other exotic snacks for tourists.

SKY BAR

The Sky Bar at Lebua State Tower sits 64 floors and 250 meters above the city and being the highest rooftop bar in the city with its 360° panoramic views the bar has probably the best view over the city of Bangkok and a great place to be when the sun is setting over the Chao Phraya River.

VANILLA SKY

Vanilla Sky Rooftop Bar sits 36 stories up on top of the Compass Skyview Hotel about a five-minute walk from the BTS at Phrom Phong. The bar offers fantastic views and exotic cocktails and is one of the city's hottest nightlife spots, as well as one of the best rooftop bars in Bangkok.

ABOVE ELEVEN

Above Eleven Bar at the Fraser Suites Hotel is a 3-storey rooftop bar located on the 33rd floor of Sukhumvit Soi 11. The bar's view of downtown Bangkok is one of the best of all the sky bars as you get 180° panoramic views of lit-up Bangkok City below on an evening. The rooftop bar resembles an urban city park with trees and a maze and has a fantastic view of the Bangkok skyline. The restaurant offers Peruvian and a Japanese Cuisine called Nikkei served as both main courses and snacks.

SOI COWBOY.

There are 3 main red-light districts in Bangkok: Soi Cowboy which is the most famous, Nana Plaza which is for your more enthusiastic punter and Patpong.

Soi Cowboy is the most well-known red-light district in the whole of Thailand. The area got its name from T.G. "Cowboy" Edwards, a retired African American airman who served in the Vietnam War and went on to open one of the first ex-pat bars in the area in 1977. He got his nickname because he invariably wore a cowboy hat and western cowboy shirts. It's a great place to soak up the red-light atmosphere and it's not compulsory to buy a lady drink or take one back to your place, it's just a fun night out. Soi Cowboy is another short street in Bangkok with a big reputation. The 150-meter-long soi has 40, mostly go-go bars and caters to the thousands of tourists and locals who walk down the street each night, some out of curiosity others to sample the wares.

NANA PLAZA

Nana Plaza promotes itself as the "World's Largest Adult Playground" Unlike the better-known Soi Cowboy or Patpong, Nana Plaza is more for your serious lady bar hoppers and you don't get many curious tourists strolling around looking to take photos or selfies to send to their friends back home to show what a naughty holiday they are having. Nana Plaza was originally built as a shopping centre and occupies a three-story commercial building in the Khlong Toei District of Bangkok and is about 300 meters from the BTS Skytrain's Nana Station. The ground floor is mostly open-air beer bars, while the shows and the go-go bars are located on the 1st floor including Spanky's, Angewitch, and Fantasia a Go-Go. G-Spot, Cassanova and Temptations are among the most popular for their ladyboy shows. Three short-time hotels operate on the top floor of the plaza. who rent out rooms by the hour or longer depending on your stamina and how deep your pockets are, to patrons to take a bargirl for sex.

PATPONG

Patpong is the oldest red-light district in Bangkok where Thailand's go-go culture started and gets its name from the family that owned much of the area's property, the Patpongpanich who were immigrants from Hainan Island, China, who purchased land in the area in 1946. The area gained popularity in the late 1960s when US soldiers came to Bangkok on Rand R from their tour of duty in Vietnam and bars with bar girls started to spring up to cater for their needs. Patpong consists of two parallel streets surrounded by the well-known Patpong night market. There are More than 20 go-go bars within the complex.

THE FOOD IN BANGKOK

Bangkok is truly a foodie's paradise; from sweet, spicy, sour and exotic Thai food like soul-warming bowls of ramen and spicy papaya salad, to big juicy American burgers and BBQ ribs, Bangkok has something for everyone. So where do you start with eating out in Bangkok? Rumour has it that Bangkok has more food outlets per square mile than anywhere else in the world. Everywhere you look there are noodle stands roadside barbecues, curry shops, chicken stalls and roti stalls and most of the large shopping centres have cheap street food courts where you can eat local street food for less than 100 Baht. Then you have the innumerable Thai restaurants you will find everywhere when travelling around the city and suburbs. Add to those the thousands of restaurants represented by just about every country in the world the range of options is eye-watering, not to mention mouthwatering. The prices will vary depending on where in the city you want to go, and how much you want to spend. For about 40 Baht you can get grilled chicken and rice or papaya salad at a market or roadside stall. A meal for two at a nice mid-range restaurant will set you back between 650 to 900 Baht + drinks. The 5-star (your anniversary-type dinner) is around 3000 Baht or more.

There are literally hundreds of food markets selling every type of meat from beef steak to crocodile steak, fruit and vegetables both Asian and Western and seafood. You can also sample insects such as fried crickets, ants, BBQ scorpions, silkworms and bamboo worms if you're brave enough to try them.

Then you have the big supermarkets Big C and Tesco Lotus in

most areas as well as the 7-11 shops, Family Marts and mom-and-pop stores on every street.

BANGKOK'S HOSPITALS AND MEDICAL FACILITIES

Thailand had over one million medical tourists in 2022 and the amount spent was estimated to be around 24 billion Thai baht. The majority of them had procedures done in Bangkok so if that many people flew in from all over the world for medical procedures, the hospitals must be very professional and organised with first-rate doctors, nurses and auxiliary staff. Yes, they come here because the treatment is more affordable than in their own country, but they wouldn't do that unless they had 100% faith in the hospitals, doctors and surgeons. With so many private and public hospitals in Bangkok, you should have no problem finding one that fits your medical needs. You rarely find doctor's surgeries in Thailand as you do in most Western countries but they do have clinics that cater for most people's medical needs. But in Bangkok, there is a doctor's surgery similar to what you may have had in your own country run by an English doctor, Dr Donna Robinson it's called the Med Consult Clinic and is used by many ex-pats and Thais alike. Bangkok has far too many hospitals to list them all but here are a few of the more popular ones. Hospitals in Bangkok include:
BNH Hospital
Samitivej Sukhumvit Hospital
Bumrungrad International Hospital
The Bangkok Christian Hospital
Phyathai Hospital
Praram 9 Hospital
Saint Louis Hospital
Central General Hospital
Vibhavadi Hospital
Many of the doctors in these hospitals will have attended university or medical school in the West and are highly skilled;

they will almost certainly be able to speak English.

THE DOWNSIDES OF LIVING IN BANGKOK.

AIR POLLUTION

Not everything is great about living in Bangkok, as with most large cities you will have to learn to live with the smog from the high volume of traffic pollution. Bangkok at certain times of the year is the second-most congested city in the world after Mexico City. The main factors of Bangkok's air pollution problem can be put down to the exhaust fumes from the city's suffocating traffic as well as the agricultural burning in the surrounding areas. Other factors that contribute to the air pollution are due to construction work and factory emissions around the city. The pollution can spike to alarming levels and is particularly bad for young children the elderly, and people with respiratory diseases, such as asthma, **emphysema and bronchitis.**

THE TRAFFIC

Bangkok has 10.67 million registered vehicles and in 2023 alone, there were 68 thousand new registered vehicles so there are more and more vehicles on the road every year. This contributes hugely to air pollution but it also makes Bangkok a nightmare to drive within the city and unless you take the trains or underground rail systems it can sometimes take ages to get to where you want to be and parking can be a problem.

BANGKOK IS ONE BIG CONCRETE JUNGLE

If you are not used to living in a big city then Bangkok could be quite a shock to the system as it is comparable to New York for its skyscrapers and infrastructure. Everywhere you go within the city you will be surrounded by buildings and people. Bangkok does have some beautiful green areas and parks to escape the crowds, including Benjakitti Park, Benjasiri Park, Chatuchak Park, Queen Sirikit Park and the famous Lumphini Park. Many people like the thrill of living in big cities but it's not for everyone...me included

BANGKOK IS VERY HOT AND HUMID

Unlike smaller towns and beach towns, being surrounded by concrete and emissions from thousands of vehicles the heat tends to be overbearing in Bangkok with little escape from it when outdoors.

BEING OVERCHARGED

The Bangkok taxi drivers are notorious for overcharging customers, more so if you are an expat. Also, dual pricing is common in Thailand and Bangkok is no exception to the rule. Dual pricing is where they charge more for a foreigner to enter an attraction or venue or buy produce than they do for a Thai person. The premise being that all farang in Thailand must be rich so they can afford it.

PHUKET

CHAPTER FOUR

PHUKET

Phuket was the first place I ever visited in Thailand, so it holds special memories for me. I came here in 1983, 41 years ago on a ship that I was working on as a chef. It was a lot different 41 years ago than it is today. Air travel was expensive, and backpackers, sex tourism and medical tourism hadn't been invented. The Brits were still going to Blackpool or were discovering The Costa Blanca, Torremolinos and Benidorm as a holiday destination for the first time. But it was mainly the rich, and because of Thailand's proximity to the lands down under, nomadic Aussies and Kiwis who ventured to Thailand back in those days. Thankfully for Phuket's future bar girls, massage parlours and Thailand tourism industry, people's perspective on where to holiday changed years later, when airfares dropped and wages went up and someone invented backpacks. Just like Koh Samui and other tourist destinations Phuket suffered greatly during the three years of the Covid pandemic but since Thailand opened up again without the Covid entry restrictions a year ago, Phuket is getting back on track to hopefully how it used to be in its pre covid days. Today, Phuket is a mixture of what I would have liked when I was a young twenty-year-old and what I like now as a retiree. Patong's Bangla Road would have been a dream come true when I was twenty. Now for me at seventy-two it's a bit over the top. I still go there occasionally, to meet friends or just to look, and imagine I am twenty again. It's full of tourists and traffic; the beaches are sometimes unclean with lots of flotsam and jetsam washed up from God knows where. You can't walk more than a few meters in town without being tormented, by someone offering you a massage, a new suit or a Tuk-Tuk. Having said that, Patong is great for the tourism industry, and if you're only coming here as a tourist for a week or two it would be quite enjoyable. The majority of retirees who live in Patong are single males, for obvious reasons. Most retiree couples or singles that prefer a quieter existence live in areas such as Kata and Karon both of which are now large Russian tourism destinations. Other popular retiree destinations are the beach suburbs of Surin, Kamala and Laguna as well as Phuket town. In 2017 when I retired to Thailand, I chose Rawai to live in and rented a house there for six months as Rawai seemed to have everything that I needed. It was only a few minutes' drive to the quiet and secluded Nai Harn Beach, a ten-minute drive to Kata Beach, another five minutes to Karon Beach and close to large shopping centres when needed and about a thirty-minute drive to Phuket town. After the initial six months, I decided that Phuket was not for me so I moved on to Koh Samui. But everyone is different so it may suit your circumstances and may well be worth taking a look at. One of the good things about living on the island of Phuket is that unlike Koh Samui and other islands in Thailand, you don't have to depend on a ferry to go on or off the island as Phuket is connected to the mainland by a causeway so you can drive on and off 24 hours a day seven days a week.

PHUKET

FACTS ABOUT PHUKET
- Population: Phuket has a population of over 450,000

- Temperature/Seasons: Phuket has a tropical monsoon climate, with average temperatures of 28°C to 32°C all year round. The island has two seasons. The wet season is from May until October and the hot season is between November and April.
- Phuket lies 827 kilometres southwest of Bangkok.
- Phuket is the largest island in Thailand and covers an area of 543 square kilometres.
- Phuket was once called Jungceylon which is the name of a large international shopping centre in Patong on the island
- Phuket is home to one of the biggest Buddha statues in Thailand, Big Buddha, which sits 45 meters in height on Nakkerd Hill, overlooking the Andaman Sea.
- The name Phuket was derived from the Malay word Bukit which means hill and is called so because of the island's mountain ranges.
- Phuket is not only an island but also a province of Thailand.

THE WEATHER IN PHUKET

November to February is the coolest season and also the busiest tourist season. March to May is generally the hottest and June to October is the wet season. It's a good idea for any retiree to have an indoor hobby that can be done from home during the wet season as you can spend a lot of time indoors at that time of the year. Most of the wet season, it doesn't rain all day, but when it rains it is monsoon-type rain.

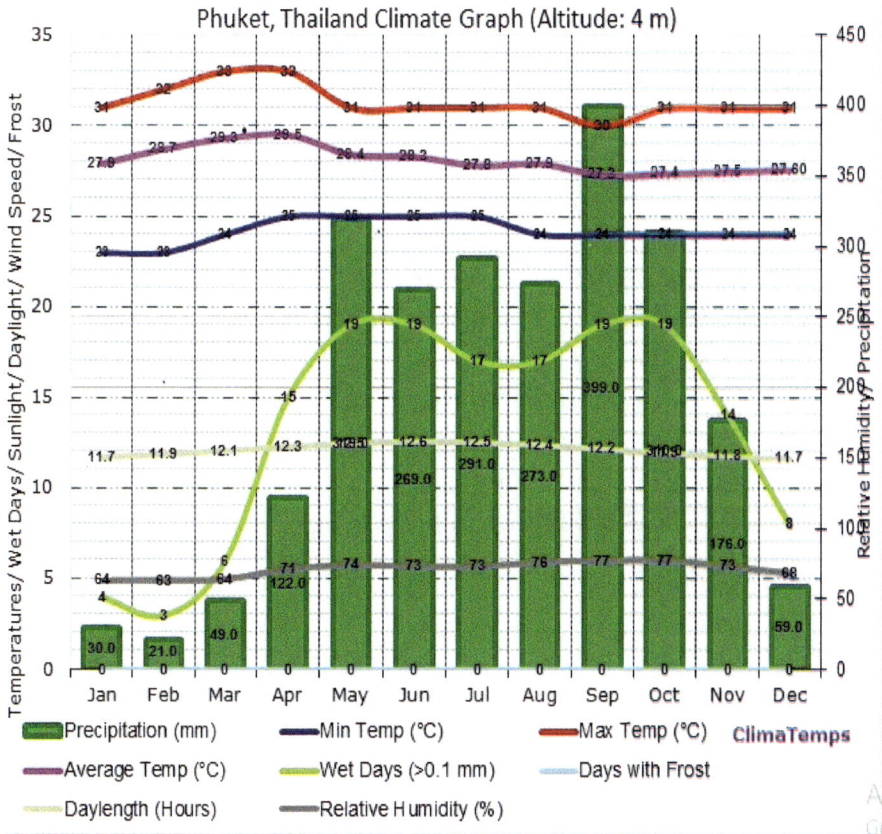

Courtesy of www.travelfish.org

THE COST OF LIVING IN PHUKET

Consumer Prices in Pattaya are 12.3% lower than in Bangkok (without rent)

Consumer Prices Including Rent in Pattaya are 18.5% lower than in Bangkok

Rent Prices in Pattaya are 34.7% lower than in Bangkok

Restaurant Prices in Pattaya are 3.4% higher than in Bangkok

Groceries Prices in Pattaya are 2.5% lower than in Bangkok

Local Purchasing Power in Pattaya is 9.7% lower than in Bangkok

The cost of living in Phuket is quite high when compared to most other areas of Thailand because Phuket is such a popular tourist destination with a busy international airport with direct flights from many Western countries and with the influx of foreign tourists that has pushed the prices up over the years, though during the Covid times the prices plummeted as they did in most tourist areas in Thailand or for that matter the world. Today Phuket is still ridiculously cheap when compared to most Western countries. You can get a fully furnished and equipped condo with a pool for around 20,000 Baht a month excluding electricity and water.

✂ Restaurants

Meal, Inexpensive Restaurant	150.00 ฿
Meal for 2 People, Mid-range Restaurant, Three-course	1,122.85 ฿
McMeal at McDonalds (or Equivalent Combo Meal)	250.00 ฿
Domestic Beer (0.5 liter draught)	97.50 ฿
Imported Beer (0.33 liter bottle)	110.00 ฿
Cappuccino (regular)	81.97 ฿
Coke/Pepsi (0.33 liter bottle)	26.33 ฿
Water (0.33 liter bottle)	15.36 ฿

🛒 Markets

Milk (regular), (1 liter)	53.54 ฿
Loaf of Fresh White Bread (500g)	54.75 ฿
Rice (white), (1kg)	51.25 ฿
Eggs (regular) (12)	73.89 ฿
Local Cheese (1kg)	602.00 ฿
Chicken Fillets (1kg)	91.09 ฿
Beef Round (1kg) (or Equivalent Back Leg Red Meat)	311.00 ฿
Apples (1kg)	110.57 ฿
Banana (1kg)	38.12 ฿
Oranges (1kg)	61.17 ฿
Tomato (1kg)	50.29 ฿
Potato (1kg)	44.12 ฿
Onion (1kg)	40.29 ฿
Lettuce (1 head)	35.00 ฿
Water (1.5 liter bottle)	16.33 ฿
Bottle of Wine (Mid-Range)	600.00 ฿
Domestic Beer (0.5 liter bottle)	57.32 ฿
Imported Beer (0.33 liter bottle)	81.57 ฿
Cigarettes 20 Pack (Marlboro)	142.00 ฿

🚗 Transportation

One-way Ticket (Local Transport)	40.00 ฿
Monthly Pass (Regular Price)	380.24 ฿
Taxi Start (Normal Tariff)	100.00 ฿
Taxi 1km (Normal Tariff)	50.00 ฿
Taxi 1hour Waiting (Normal Tariff)	450.00 ฿
Gasoline (1 liter)	42.35 ฿
Volkswagen Golf 1.4 90 KW Trendline (Or Equivalent New Car)	700,000.00 ฿
Toyota Corolla Sedan 1.6l 97kW Comfort (Or Equivalent New Car)	962,500.00 ฿

🏠 Utilities (Monthly)

Basic (Electricity, Heating, Cooling, Water, Garbage) for 85m2 Apartment	3,648.21 ฿
Mobile Phone Monthly Plan with Calls and 10GB+ Data	511.56 ฿
Internet (60 Mbps or More, Unlimited Data, Cable/ADSL)	506.58 ฿

🚴 Sports And Leisure

Fitness Club, Monthly Fee for 1 Adult	2,072.22 ฿
Tennis Court Rent (1 Hour on Weekend)	400.00 ฿
Cinema, International Release, 1 Seat	300.00 ฿

🛒 Childcare

Preschool (or Kindergarten), Full Day, Private, Monthly for 1 Child	15,816.67 ฿
International Primary School, Yearly for 1 Child	367,000.00 ฿

👕 Clothing And Shoes

1 Pair of Jeans (Levis 501 Or Similar)	1,548.33 ฿
1 Summer Dress in a Chain Store (Zara, H&M, ...)	1,141.43 ฿
1 Pair of Nike Running Shoes (Mid-Range)	3,757.14 ฿
1 Pair of Men Leather Business Shoes	2,500.00 ฿

🛏 Rent Per Month

Apartment (1 bedroom) in City Centre	18,458.33 ฿
Apartment (1 bedroom) Outside of Centre	16,250.00 ฿
Apartment (3 bedrooms) in City Centre	59,090.91 ฿
Apartment (3 bedrooms) Outside of Centre	50,500.00 ฿

🏢 Buy Apartment Price

Price per Square Meter to Buy Apartment in City Centre	101,250.00 ฿
Price per Square Meter to Buy Apartment Outside of Centre	67,000.00 ฿

Courtesy of www.numbeo.com

WHAT DOES PHUKET OFFER FOR EXPATS LIVING THERE?

It's hard to put a figure on how many expats live in Phuket as it's such a transient community with tourists regularly arriving on and off the island from many overseas destinations. I have heard estimates of between twenty and thirty thousand. It's not hard to play spot the expats; they are so different to the tourists. You just have to look at the people and you can say to yourself he lives here or he's on holiday. I can't put my finger on how you can tell. Perhaps it's just their confident attitude or where they seem to know where they are going. There are lots of expat social clubs but I haven't found one with their own building. I'm not saying there isn't one, if there is I just haven't found it. There's the Phuket Beach Meetup Club. The Grumpy Old Men's Society, whose meetings are held on the first and third Monday of every month, the main criteria for being a member of the club is its men only, it doesn't matter their age, but it helps if they're prone to grumpiness now and then (sounds like my kind of club). Phuket Expats Club, Expats in Phuket Meet up Club and Chicky Net a women's only expat club.

***See Useful Website pages at the end of
this book for expat club links**

PLACES TO GO AND THINGS TO DO IN PHUKET

POPULAR BEACHES OF PHUKET

- **Patong Beach**
- **Karon Beach**
- **Kata Beach**
- **Kamala Beach**

- **Bang Tao Beach**
- **Nai Thon Beach**
- **Nai Harn Beach**
- **Mai Khao Beach**
- **Freedom Beach**
- **Ya Nui Beach**
- **Banana Beach**

PATONG BEACH

Patong is the main beach on the west coast of Phuket, and the beach is probably the busiest though not the best beach on the island. As it is the beach that is closest to the red-light district of Patong, it can also seem quite seedy and gaudy, though it is relatively quiet on the northern end of the beach. This is not your quiet relaxing beach, as you are surrounded by hotels, shopping malls, bars, restaurants and many tourist outlets trying to sell you everything imaginable including women and ladyboys who also ply their trade along the boardwalk during the daytime hours. It's well worth seeing but there are better more relaxing beaches all around Phuket.

KARON BEACH

With 3.5 kilometres of golden sand Karon Beach or Had Karon as it is called by the locals is the second-longest beach in Phuket and one of the most popular beaches on the island. The beach is an impressive sight with its coconut trees dotted along the foreshore and the Andaman Sea breaking on its sandy beach. Karon has long been among the most popular of Phuket's beaches, along with neighbouring Patong Beach, to the north and Kata Beach to the south. If you are in need of refreshments, just cross the main road that runs parallel to the beach and there are many bars, restaurants and food outlets.

KATA BEACH

Kata Beach is a 1.5-km strip of golden sand and along with Karon Beach is considered one of the most popular beaches in Phuket due to its beach facilities such as sun loungers and umbrellas for rent. Wandering vendors roam the beach selling ice creams, fresh fruits, whole coconuts, BBQ sweetcorn, sarongs, sunglasses beachwear and other clothing. At the southern end of the beach, on the main road, you will find shops, restaurants and street vendor stalls selling a variety of snacks, fruits, juices, spicey Issan sausages, Som Tam and many other foods as well as clothing and beach accessories.

KAMALA BEACH

Kamala Beach is located between Surin Beach and Patong Beach. The beach is the main reason that many tourists flock to Kamala Beach as it's long and wide and fringed with casuarinas and coconut trees lining the beach. The Kamala area was severely impacted during the 2004 tsunami and a lot of the area had to be rebuilt in its wake. Before the tidal wave hit Phuket, Kamala was a small sleepy fishing village with a mostly Muslim population After its re-birth Kamala then became much better known as a tourist destination on the island. As in many built-up beach towns in Phuket, all along the beach road, you will find international restaurants, food vendors and market stalls.

BANG TAO BEACH

Bang Tao Beach is 6 kilometres in length, making it Phuket's longest beach as well as one of the best beaches to capture a stunning sunset over the Andaman Sea. The northern end of the beach is usually quite deserted but the southern end where the area has become home to some of Phuket's most luxurious resorts is sometimes a little busier. The beach lies halfway between Phuket Airport and Patong on the island's west coast.

NAI THON BEACH

Nai Thon Beach is one of Phuket's hidden gems as it is located quite far from the main road and tends to remain quiet, as most tourists like the glitzier more popular beaches. The beach is long and wide with soft white sand, perfect for those in search of a more peaceful relaxing place to spend the day, with just a few restaurants, food stalls and shops scattered nearby for convenience.

NAI HARN BEACH
Nai Harn Beach is a very popular beach on the island and as such can get busy, especially in the high season. Located in the South of the island close to the popular town of Rawai the beach is surrounded by green hills and dotted with small islands out at sea. Nai Harn Beach is a complete contrast from the more touristy beach areas on the west coast such as Patong, Karon and Kata. The beach is in a sheltered bay where sailing and fishing boats sit anchored in calm waters. Just behind the park that surrounds the beach, you will find some Thai restaurants and market stalls.

MAI KHAO BEACH
Mai Khao Beach is on the northwest coast of Phuket adjacent to Phuket International Airport. This 11-kilometre stretch of beach is part of the Sirinat National Park. Being a long way out of town and away from the tourist strips Mai Khao Beach is a lot less visited compared to Phuket's popular beaches like Kata, Patong and Karon. Mai Khao Beach is renowned for being one of the best places on the island for plane spotting and many tourists come here to get selfies and photos of the planes that seem to fly just a few meters above your head as they come into land at the Phuket Airport.

FREEDOM BEACH
Freedom Beach is another beautiful beach in Phuket, with incredibly soft white sand and clear blue waters. Surprisingly, it's just next to the crowded Patong beach, but despite being so close it is relatively quiet. This is because: there are only two ways you can access the beach, by boat or from the top of the hill, down a very steep slope.

YA NUI BEACH

Located in the southern part of Phuket close to Promthep Cape, Ya Nui is a popular beach if you are looking for a smaller and quieter beach rather than the larger more touristy beaches on the island. The beach is perfect for diving and snorkelling enthusiasts with its crystal clear and normally calm waters. If you stay until early evening, you can also watch the sunset over the magnificent Promthep Cape from this beach which is something not to be missed.

BANANA BEACH

Banana Beach is another beach not to be missed if you're a beach lover. The beach is located in northwest Phuket, a little way out of town and close to Freedom Beach which you can reach via a long-tail boat or by a steep hike down from the roadside. There are so many more beaches all around Phuket waiting for you to discover them.

As with its smaller sister island Koh Samui, it's hard to know where to start when it comes to deciding what to do in Phuket and even more so because Phuket is much bigger than Koh Samui. Patong is the main area of Phuket for tourists which is great if you like the razmataz of a bustling town but the real beauty of Phuket lies in its beaches and Phang Nga Bay. On Boxing Day the 26th of December 2004, the west coast of Phuket was struck by the tsunami that devasted the coastal areas of many Asian countries. Patong was one of the worst affected areas of Phuket, although the destruction was not as bad as its nearby neighbour Khao Lak where the official death toll was 4,000. Still, this is considered to be an underestimate, with unofficial estimates reaching as high as ten thousand due to the high number of undocumented Myanmar migrants who were unaccounted for. Patong and the rest of the island have risen from the ashes and rebuilt themselves.

BIG BUDDHA

It is called The Great Buddha of Phuket but most people know it as just Big Buddha and it sits at the summit of Nakkerd Hill which is situated between Chalong and Kata. The Buddha statue depicts Gautama or Lord Buddha in a sitting position and is an impressive 45 meters tall and 25 meters wide and is visible from just about anywhere in the southern part of Phuket. Big Buddha is accessed via a winding, 6-kilometre road and when you reach the peak, you will be rewarded with sweeping 360° panoramic views of the island and the Andaman Sea. Big Buddha took more than 10 years to build and the temple was finally completed in 2014. is open 7 days a week from 8.00 am to 7.30 pm. There is no entry fee though donations are appreciated to help with the upkeep of the temple.

OLD PHUKET TOWN

Phuket Town is often neglected by tourists who tend to come to the island mainly for the beaches, nightlife, lady bars and perhaps a visit to Big Buddha. But long before tourism arrived in Phuket in the early 1970s it was an island of rubber trees and lucrative tin mines. Because of this Phuket absorbed many aspects of the varying cultures who over the centuries arrived on the island to work the rubber plantations and mine the tin, from countries such as China, India, Indonesia and Portugal. Phuket Old Town is known for its brightly painted classical time-honoured Sino-Portuguese buildings many of which have been converted into shops, hotels, restaurants, and museums. The pick of them would be the well-preserved row along Soi Rommanee, Krabi Road, Dibuk Road and Thalang Road. There are many restaurants and coffee shops in the area to keep you well-watered and fed whilst you are wandering through the colourful streets and if you come at the weekend, you will be able to take in the atmosphere of Chatuchak Weekend Market and maybe find some bargains once you get past the fake brand name designer clothing, bags and counterfeit watches.

PUM THAI RESTAURANT & COOKING SCHOOL

Perhaps you have always loved the exotic flavours of Thai food or maybe you have acquired a taste for it in your home country as everywhere you go in the world you will find Thai restaurants, so you may want to learn some authentic cookery skills while you are living in Phuket. Pum Thai Restaurant & Cooking School in Patong is open daily and offers four cookery classes to choose from. A quick 90 minutes, 4 hours, 5 hours and 6-plus hours. The courses range from simple introductions that give you a taste of the basics of Thai cooking to intensive classes that can turn you into a Master Chef. There are many Thai cookery schools in Phuket and most tourist islands and towns in Thailand (just do a Google search). This one was recommended to me as being exceptional

JUNG CEYLON SHOPPING MALL

Jungceylon Shopping Center is the major mall in Patong and one of the biggest in Phuket. The shopping mall is named after the old name of Phuket as the island was known as Jungceylon from 1545 for hundreds of years. The mall's two main stores are Robinson Ocean Jungceylon which is a huge department store selling just about everything, clothing, electronics, luggage, jewellery, cosmetics the list is endless. The other major store is Big C a huge supermarket. There are over 200 other stores within the complex plus Cinema City, a 16-lane bowling alley, food courts and the usual Western cuisines and fast-food outlets such as McDonalds and KFC

GREEN ELEPHANT SANCTUARY PARK

If you have always wanted to visit an elephant sanctuary there are a few in Phuket, the best and most ethical in my opinion is The Green Elephant Sanctuary. Elephants can be seen working and performing all over Phuket in tourism shows, but unless you head to the jungle or national parks back on the mainland you won't find them as happy and contented as those Elephants who call Green Elephant Sanctuary home. By visiting here, you will learn about the elephant's behaviour and the role of elephants in Thai culture and you will get to know each of the elephant's personal stories and how they came to end up in the sanctuary. You will also have the opportunity to get hands-on with feeding, washing and swimming with these majestic gentle giants. Be careful when visiting any elephant sanctuaries here because Phuket has several elephant sanctuaries that are not true sanctuaries but more like tourist attractions.

Phang Nga Bay

No trip to Phuket is complete without a trip to Phang Nga Bay. Phang Nga Bay is a 400-square-kilometre gulf that surrounds Phuket's east coastline in the Ao Phang Nga Marine National Park. Much the same as Vietnam's Halong Bay, Phang Nga Bay is famous for its mystical limestone cliffs that are scattered throughout the bay. There are many ways to explore Phang Nga. You can take a languid cruise on a Chinese junk, a traditional longboat, a speed boat or by canoe. All around the bay are hundreds of caves hidden within the limestone cliffs that are accessible by boat. The most famous of the many islands in the bay is Ko Ta Pu, or James Bond Island as it is also called due to the 1974, 007 movie The Man with the Golden Gun being filmed on the island. James Bond Island is located about 25 kilometres northeast of Phuket Island so unless you are very fit the canoe option of visiting the island would probably be out of the question. Ko Ta Pu also featured in the 1997 James Bond film Tomorrow Never Dies, in which Phang Nga Bay served as a stand-in for Vietnam's Ha Long Bay.

WAT CHALONG

As in all of Thailand, Buddhist Temples play a big part in the daily lives of the people of Phuket and locals and tourists alike come to take in the beauty and mystical aura of the many Buddhist temples that are scattered across the island. Big

Buddha may be the number-one temple choice for tourists but for Thais, Wat Chalong is top of the list. Built at the beginning of the 19th century, Wat Chalong is the largest and most visited Buddhist temple in Phuket. The most iconic building on the temple grounds is a 60-meter-tall stupa with a fragment of bone reputed to have come from Buddha. When you enter the stupa, you will find gold statues of Buddha and beautiful paintings on the walls and ceilings that depict the life of Lord Buddha. On reaching the summit of the stupa you will be rewarded with panoramic views of Phuket and beyond below.

KARON VIEWPOINT

Karon viewpoint is located south of Kata Noi Beach with stunning views out over the Andaman Sea and is one of the best and most frequented viewpoints in Phuket. Strategically located between Nai Harn and Kata Noi beaches you can take in views of Kata Yai, Kata Noi and Karon beaches below. The viewpoint is about a 10-minute drive from Kata Beach and is open 24 hours so you can watch the sun rise and set from the lookout.

WHAT TO DO WHEN THE SUN GOES DOWN IN PHUKET?

Phuket's nightlife, just like Pattaya is well known for being extreme and outlandish but Patong is the undisputed nightlife hub of Phuket and the beating heart of Patong is Bangla Road. Kata, Rawai and Karon have a similar but not-so-in-your-face nightlife scene. Having close to half a million people living on the island plus the influx of the millions of foreign tourists that flock to the island every year for sun, sea and entertainment it's not all about the lady bars, as the whole of the island has restaurants and food outlets to suit every taste and every budget.

PATONG

Bangla Road is lined with bars and nightclubs with neon lights and pulsing dance music everywhere you walk. All along the

400-metre strip, you will find go-go dancers and pole dancers on stages, while on the street at the front of the bars, in skimpy outlets leaving nothing to the imagination their co-workers stand trying to entice you into their bars by offering you happy hour drinks at bargain prices and much more should you want to take one of them home. The side streets adjoining Bangla Road are filled with the same and there are also dozens of massage shops offering every type of massage imaginable. Don't worry if you're not interested in sampling what's on offer, it's not compulsory but it's well worth going to Bangla Road just to take in the atmosphere and see how the other half lives.

SIMON CABARET

On the Southern end of Patong lies Simon Cabaret which has been a part of Phuket's entertainment scene for over 33 years. The venue offers an evening of live music, dance and comedy performances by a cast of transgender entertainers, performed in a 3000-seat theatre. The adult show is a spectacular display of choreography, outrageous costumes, and fun. There's a shopping street where you can buy souvenirs and the show incorporates a huge buffet restaurant At the end of the 70-minute show, the performers pose for photos outside with members of the audience for a small fee.

MUAY THAI (THAI BOXING)

Patong is a great place to see live Muay Thai matches. It has 2 stadiums. Patong Boxing Stadium and Bangla Boxing Stadium.

At Patong Boxing Stadium matches are usually held every Monday, Thursday and Saturday nights. With Bangla Boxing Stadium being in the main redlight district of Bangla Road many of the fighters are foreign boxers who have come to Thailand to learn the art of Muay Thai they also sometimes have women's Muay Thai matches. Bangla Boxing Stadium features regular Thai boxing fights 3 nights a week, on Wednesdays, Fridays and Sundays.

KAMALA

Kamala runs at a lot slower pace than its southern neighbour Patong which is why it is more frequented by couples and families. There are quite a few bars and some lady bars scattered around the town.

PHUKET FANTASEA

Phuket FantaSea is a 60-acre cultural evening theme park, packed with a multitude of activities and entertainment venues featuring several attractions such as a Thai cultural theatrical show, a themed buffet restaurant, and a shopping street. The Fantasea show constructed in ancient Khmer-style architecture, displays the beauty, myths, mystery and culture of Thailand entwined with a Las Vegas-style show featuring elephants, monkeys and tigers. The 4,000-seat theme Golden Kinnaree International Buffet Restaurant offers both Thai and International cuisine which gives a feeling of dining in a royal palace.

CAFÉ DEL MAR

Café del Mar Phuket is a classy beach club and an offshoot of the world-famous brand in Ibiza Spain. With its high-quality settings and great music, it brings a sophisticated party atmosphere to the northern end of Kamala Beach.

Vanilla Sky Bar & Gastro Pub

Vanilla Sky Bar & Gastro Pub occupies the rooftop of Cape Sienna Phuket Hotel a 5-star resort along Phuket's Millionaire Mile in the southern end of Kamala Beach. Here you can sit while sipping a cocktail and watching the sun go down over the Andaman Sea. The bar boasts a cocktail lounge, snooker room and a restaurant

DIAVOLO AT THE PARESA RESORT

Another stunning bar within a resort in Kamala is Diavolo at the Paresa Resort just down the soi from The Vanilla Sky

Bar. The restaurant has an outdoor terrace perched on a cliff with the Andaman Sea some 50 meters below.

AUSSIE PUB

The glitzy bars in the upmarket hotels are quite pricy but if you're just looking to quench your thirst and grab a bite to eat without paying for the view the Aussie Pub may suit your needs. This iconic pub is a 2-storey nightlife venue on the Kamala main road. The downstairs bar features many large-screen TVs showing live sports events and a pool table. On the 2nd floor is the restaurant area with an extensive selection of international dishes and pub grub.

PHUKET TOWN

SIAM NIRAMIT

Siam Niramit is a Thai cultural show narrating over 700 years of Thailand's heritage, history, mythology and Thai traditions. The parklands that surround the theatre recreate traditional Thai villages from around Thailand where wandering performers demonstrate traditional music and dance. There's also a floating market and of course souvenir shops. This cultural show does not incorporate animals into its show hence the performance is more ethical and authentic. The park is located on the Bypass Road in the northwestern area of Phuket Town

SIMON STAR

Simon Star in Phuket Town is the younger sister of Simon Cabaret in Patong. The massive theatre is located near Samkong, in the northern area of the city. The flamboyant dancers are feminine and glamorous ladyboys, known as "kathoey" in Thai and they wear glamourous gowns and perform an entertaining ladyboy cabaret show that is fun to watch as they often interact with their audience. With their hourglass figures, flashy gowns and feminine elegant ways, it can be hard to believe that they were born male. Be warned their humour can be bawdy and if you are a male and sitting close to the stage you may be chosen as the object of their jokes, but it is all in fun. After the show, you can have your photo taken with your favourite dancer or a group of them for a small tip.

THE TIMBER HUT

Timber Hut Is a 2-storey building on Yaowarat Road, at the northern end of Phuket Old Town and has been a long-established venue in Phuket Town for over 30 years. Made up of two floors, each with its own bar, with the top bar overlooking the band playing below. The decor is a mixture of Thai and Western styles with many flags draped from the ceiling and strategically placed video screens throughout the bar area. The bar hosts nightly live music playing both international and Thai favourites to please both the locals and tourists. Both food and drinks are sold at affordable prices. At one time Mick Jagger was spotted having a drink at Timber Hut so it must have something good going for it.

KARON

Most of the nightlife experiences in Karon are centred around the bars off Patak Road, near the northern traffic circle, or Luang Poh Chuan Road which is also known in the area as Bangla Plaza due to its lively bars and clubs. Along Beach Road, there are many hotel bars and lounges with a more relaxing atmosphere.

BANGLA PLAZA

Bangla Plaza has several decent bars and restaurants many of them are lady bars with a few lady boys to make up the numbers. Some of the popular are Winner Bar, My Way Bar, Black Cat Bar, Nan Jinda Bar and Night Flower Bar.

SOI ONE MAN

Close to the centre of Karon is a small street called Soi One Man, which is filled with many lady bars. Cherry Bar, Lucky Bar, Mona Bar, and Happy Elephant Bar to name but a few.

HEAVEN RESTAURANT & BAR

Heaven Restaurant & Bar sits below the famous Karon Viewpoint and another bar comes restaurant with breathtaking sunset views over the Andaman Sea from the rooftop deck and the main dining area.

THE AFTER-BEACH BAR

Up on the hillside, a few minutes' drive from Kata Beach you will find the After Beach Bar and as the name suggests the bar sits right on the beach. This trendy bar has been here for many years which is always a good sign in Thailand where businesses come and go regularly and is frequented by both local Thais and expats. In this Jamaican-themed bar and restaurant adorned with Jamaican flags, you can watch the sun setting over the Andaman Sea while listening to Bob Marley while sipping on a cocktail or a cold beer and almost believe that you are in Montego Bay in Jamaica.

KATA

Located just 15 minutes from lively crazy Patong and just south of Karon is the laid-back beach town of Kata. Kata town is quite compact and easy to get around. There are many bars and restaurants located at the north end of Kata and they eventually join up with the neighbouring town of Karon creating one long stretch of shops restaurants and bars linking the two towns.

THE WALK

There are quite a few lady bar areas on Kata Road with most of the street being the hub of the nightlife in Kata selling the usual cheap beers, loud music and friendly hostesses including The Walk which has a line of beer bars running through the centre of the complex.

SKA BAR

This iconic Ska Bar is tucked away among the huge granite boulders at the southern end of Kata Beach. Many bars in

Thailand are linked to Jamaica and Reggae music is the music of choice in this bar. Ska Bar is set on different levels linked by wooden terraces

LANA BAR

Katas Lana Bar has a fun and energetic atmosphere. The bar is famous for its large jugs of cocktails, which are served with a multitude of straws to make sharing easy. The bar has great music playing throughout the night.

KATA NIGHT MARKET

Located along Kata New Road is The Kata Night Market. it's impossible to miss the giant King Kong Gorilla and The Incredible Hulk statues dominating the market's entrances and visiting Kata would not be the same if you didn't see the Kata Night Market. The market is a domed-covered shopping area with a massive food court most of which are spicy Thai traditional foods with lots of seafood dishes. There are also many tourist-oriented stalls selling arts and crafts, clothing and souvenirs.

RAWAI

With Rawai being way down south of Phuket not many tourists visit this lovely town, probably due to its distant location. Rawai has a special place in my heart for me because Rawai was the first place that I called home when I came to Thailand to live in 2017. Rawai officially begins at Chalong Circle and halfway between Rawai and the Chalong Circle, on a soi leading down to the sea, is Friendship Beach. A long-established location for live music which is well worth a look. There is a mix of lady bars combined with ladyboys throughout Rawai predominantly on the main road leading down to the beach. Rawai Beach is known for its long-tailed boats, the Sea Gypsies Fish Market and its many seafood restaurants that stretch all along the boardwalk. To the south of Rawai sits Promthep Cape.

PROMTHEP CAPE

As the sun is setting over the Andaman Sea take in the breathtaking views from Promthep Cape a rocky headland that overlooks the coast located at the Southwestern tip of Phuket. This breathtaking sunset viewing spot is famous for its iconic lighthouse, with light beams that can be seen up to 40 kilometres out to sea. There are plenty of restaurants, coffee shops and market stalls scattered around the area if you're in need of refreshment.

LAGUNA PLAZA

The biggest and noisiest night venue in Rawai is The Laguna Night Club and Plaza which is the hottest spot in Rawai for bars, ladies and music. Located just 800 meters from Rawai Beach, the nightclub is strategically set in the back of Laguna Plaza. The plaza itself is a complex of dozens of lady bars with loud music blasting out from the different venues and beautiful Thai ladies welcoming you to their bars.

NIKITAS

Nikita's is the only bar that sits right on Rawai Beach and has always been a long-time favourite among locals, ex-pats and tourists who have discovered Rawai. With a great menu with both Thai and international dishes, views of the fishing boats leaving the harbour and magnificent sunsets it's a great place to relax after a hard day relaxing on the beach.

COCONUT

Coconut is a sports bar screening live games from around the world and sits right at the end of Rawai Beach. Their restaurant serves both Thai and international food and all-day breakfast and is a great spot to eat and drink while listening to live music in the evening.

RAWAI SEAFOOD MARKET

Rawai Seafood Market started as a small fisherman's village where you could buy the local overnight catch each day and take home to cook. Over the years the small market grew in popularity and the result is that today it's a booming busy market and food stall outlet. Here you can buy your choice of fish, crab, squid, prawns, shellfish or lobster at market price. After you select your seafood, you then pick one of the many restaurants in the market complex to cook it for you for about 100 baht per kilo. You will find that at Rawai Seafood most of the restaurants have no views which is a bit of a shame. But here is an alternative, one of the reasons I chose Rawai to live in Phuket when I first came here to live in 2017 was because of the amazing seafood outlets right on the beach on the beach road. It's an incredible culinary experience as you walk along the road and when you find the seafood stall that takes your fancy you choose your seafood, lobster, mussels, prawns, squid, whole fish, or clams from one of the many stalls opposite the beach and there's just an amazing selection to choose from that has been freshly caught overnight by local fishermen. You then choose whichever restaurant you want to cook your meal for you and how you want it cooked. Next, you go across to the beach side of the street where the restaurants have set up tables overlooking the water, order your drinks, and wait for your meal to arrive. Life doesn't get much better than that.

THE FOOD IN PHUKET

But it's not just Rawai where you will find incredible food in Phuket. Everywhere you go from one end of the island to the other you will find all types of food from around the world, as well as the usual Thailand fare. All of the beach areas have their own atmosphere when it comes to dining and Phuket town has some of the best restaurants in Thailand. Even the shopping centres have exquisite cuisine. Jung Ceylon shopping centre in Patong has over twenty top-class restaurants all with different cuisines, including Chinese, Japanese, Korean, Italian, South American, German, Mediterranean and of course Thai.

PHUKET HOSPITALS AND MEDICAL FACILITIES

Phuket has seven hospitals, some private and some run by the Thai government. With Phuket being one of the most popular tourist destinations it is rapidly becoming a primary destination for Medical Tourism in Thailand. Phuket has some outstanding quality hospitals with many Western-trained doctors.

The private hospitals are more like luxury hotels, with first-class medical facilities and luxurious rooms. As in most hospitals in Thailand tourist areas, the majority of the doctors have been educated overseas, and speak excellent English and sometimes other European languages. As in most of Thailand due to the higher costs involved in private hospitals, the majority of Thais in Phuket use the government hospitals for any medical problems they may have as they don't have doctor's surgeries here as we have at home. Government hospitals are always extremely busy, often with long waiting times to be seen. Most expats if they have the money use private hospitals to be treated. You won't have to travel far to see a dentist in Phuket. You will find dentists everywhere in all areas of Phuket.

Some of the hospitals on the island include:

Bangkok Hospital
Vichara Hospital (Government Hospital)
Dibuk Hospital
Phuket International Hospital

THE DOWNSIDES OF LIVING IN PHUKET

THE LONG DISTANCE FROM EVERYWHERE ELSE IN THAILAND:

If you are considering living in Phuket with the idea of regular travel around Thailand then you may find that the island is quite remote and restrictive when it comes to going to other areas of the country. Phuket is a twelve-hour drive to Bangkok, Pattaya is a fourteen-hour drive and Chiang Mai is a twenty-three-hour drive so the same as living in Chiang Mai and Chiang Rai you may find that you are off the beaten track. On the plus side, the Malaysian border is fairly close driving distance to Phuket as is Krabi, Khao Lak and Koh Samui and the beautiful Phi-Phi Island is just a short ferry ride away.

THE ISLAND IS OFTEN CROWDED WITH TOURISTS

Phuket has its own international airport so you can fly in directly from many countries in the world without having to fly into Bangkok first. It is estimated that over a million tourists a month come to Phuket to seek sun and sand and the nightlife and though this is great if you are on holiday, if you live in Phuket and are looking for a quiet life then sometimes it will be hard to find some peace and quiet...more so in the high season from November until February.

MORE EXPENSIVE THAN OTHER AREAS IN THAILAND

Phuket is situated a long way from Bangkok which means that getting produce to Phuket has to come by road, shipped or flown in which makes it more expensive. The costs are then passed on to the consumer so it is more expensive to live in Phuket than in places that are closer to Bangkok such as Hua Hin. The higher costs are not so noticeable for tourists as the prices are still a lot lower than in their own countries but if you are planning on living in Phuket permanently your money won't stretch as far as it would in most other areas in Thailand.

TRAFFIC AND CONGESTION

One of the good things about living on the Island of Phuket is that it is connected to the mainland by a causeway and you can drive onto the island rather than take the ferry or a flight. But it is also one of the bad things as many people drive into Phuket which means that unlike other islands in Thailand that rely on ferries and flights to bring people to their islands Phuket is full of tour buses, trucks, cars and motorbikes, which causes traffic jams and congestion. This is more so in the high tourist season but also on Buddhist holidays and Songkran, the Thai New Year in April.

FEWER CHOICES FOR TRANSPORTATION

You won't find trains in Phuket so if you want to see other areas of the country and don't want to drive then you will have to take a bus or fly. However, on the plus side, you can get the ferry to Krabi and Phi-Phi Island from Phuket.

HUA HIN

 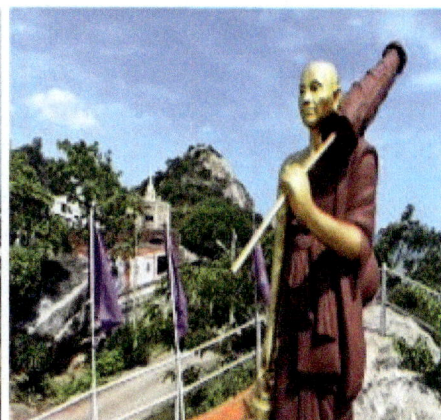

CHAPTER FIVE

HUA HIN

It is estimated that there are five thousand ex-pats living in Hua Hin and increasing all the time. With its proximity to Bangkok only being about a two-and-a-half-hour drive and about a three-and-a-half-hour train journey, though they are currently building a high-speed train line that will reduce the travel time considerably. So, it's a great place to live and within easy access to the capital city if you feel like a day out or a weekend away which is one of the reasons why I currently live here. Before Covid reared its ugly head in January 2020 there was a ferry that operated between Hua Hin and Pattaya across the Gulf of Thailand but when the tourists stopped coming to Hua Hin and Pattaya so did the ferry and to date, it has not restarted and unfortunately it probably won't start the route again.

Hua Hin has eleven world-class golf courses within easy driving distance from the city centre and the area is becoming one of the more popular destinations for retirees. Like the rest of Thailand, Hua Hin has many beautiful temples to visit. The stunning Phraya Nakhon Cave just south of Hua Hin and Pala U Waterfall is also well worth the trip it's on the south side of Kaeng Krachan National Park which borders Myanmar and is one of the largest waterfalls in the country. There is also a wonderful ornate train station at Hua Hin with trains from Bangkok arriving about eleven times a day and then departing for such faraway places as Chumphon, Surat Thani (for Koh Samui and Krabi) Hat Yai and Padang Besar on the Malaysian border. There is a jazz festival held on Hua Hin beach in June of each year. Hua Hin has always been one of the favourite retreats for the Thai Royal Family and they have a summer palace here on the outskirts of town. Half an hour's drive north from Hua Hin is the beach town of Cha Am and heading south there are some lovely beach areas for a day out if you want to get away from the tourists, such as Khao Tao, Pran Buri Beach, Khao Kalok, Sam Roi Yot and a little bit further away Ao Manao and Ban Krut in Prachuap Khiri Khan.

FACTS ABOUT HUA HIN

- Population: 85,000
- Temperature/Seasons: Hua Hin has a tropical savannah climate with three main seasons: The dry Season from November to February, the hot season from March until June and the wet season from July until October. Hua Hin has one of the lowest rainfall measurements in the country.
- Hua Hin lies approximately 220 kilometres south of Bangkok
- Hua Hin is one of the eight districts in the province of Prachuap Khiri Khan.
- Hua Hin is the home to the King of Thailand's summer palace, Maruekhathaiyawan Palace, which sits mid-way between Cha-Am and Hua Hin and was built by King Vajiravudh (Rama VI) as a seaside summer retreat in 1923.
- Hua Hin has one of the oldest and the most beautiful train stations in Thailand, which was built in 1926 to replace the original station. The main feature of the station is the royal waiting room constructed to welcome the King and the royal family when they would visit the town by train from the capital to escape Bangkok's oppressive heat.

THE HUA HIN WEATHER

Hua Hin has similar weather patterns and seasons as Koh Samui. May is the hottest month with an average temperature of 30°c the coldest is January at 26°c. The wettest month is

November. There are three seasons, the dry season December until February, the hot season March until August and the rainy season September through November.

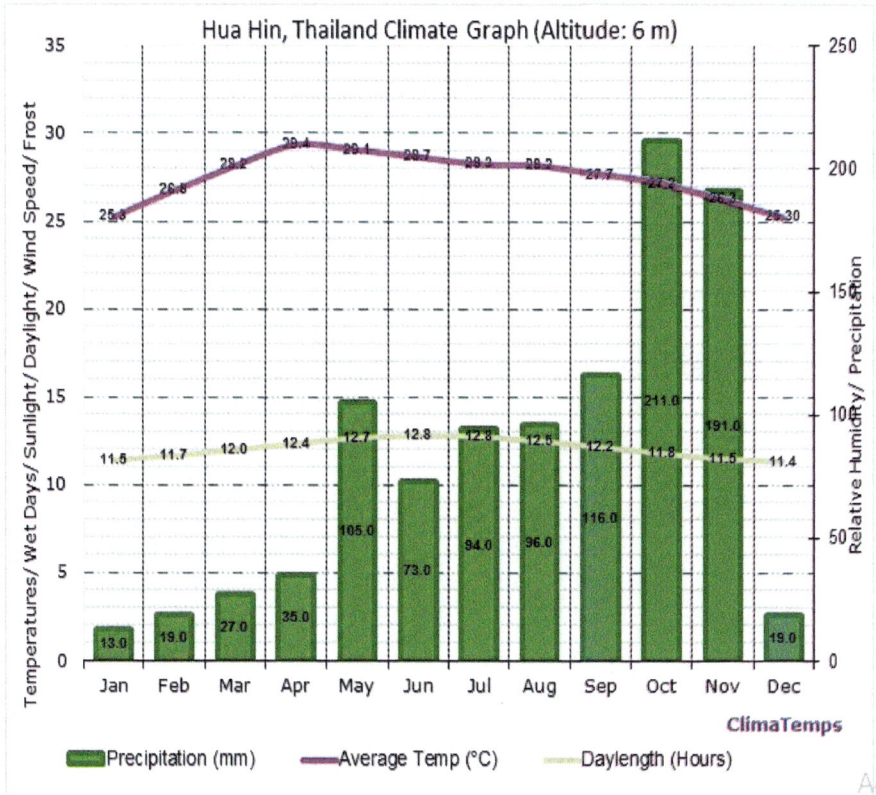

Courtesy of www.travelfish.org.com

THE HUA HIN COST OF LIVING

Hua Hin is located in the Prachuap Khiri Khan province. It is a lot cheaper city to live in compared to Bangkok, Pattaya and Phuket. It will cost you a little more to live in Hua Hin than in Chiang Mai as properties in Chiang Mai are 30% to 50% cheaper. I suppose Hua Hin is about the middle of the road for the cost of living in Thailand. But keep in mind wherever you choose to retire in Thailand it will be far cheaper to live here than in the

UK, Australia the USA or most Western countries.

Consumer Prices in Hua Hin are 24.8% lower than in Bangkok (without rent)

Consumer Prices Including Rent in Hua Hin are 30.5% lower than in Bangkok

Rent Prices in Hua Hin are 45.2% lower than in Bangkok

Restaurant Prices in Hua Hin are 3.9% lower than in Bangkok

Groceries Prices in Hua Hin are 18.0% lower than in Bangkok

Local Purchasing Power in Hua Hin is 39.6% higher than in Bangkok

✗ Restaurants

Meal, Inexpensive Restaurant	120.00 ฿
Meal for 2 People, Mid-range Restaurant, Three-course	1,000.00 ฿
McMeal at McDonalds (or Equivalent Combo Meal)	200.00 ฿
Domestic Beer (0.5 liter draught)	70.00 ฿
Imported Beer (0.33 liter bottle)	85.00 ฿
Cappuccino (regular)	55.00 ฿
Coke/Pepsi (0.33 liter bottle)	16.73 ฿
Water (0.33 liter bottle)	12.28 ฿

🛒 Markets

Milk (regular), (1 liter)	44.12 ฿
Loaf of Fresh White Bread (500g)	48.21 ฿
Rice (white), (1kg)	34.35 ฿
Eggs (regular) (12)	58.00 ฿
Local Cheese (1kg)	400.00 ฿
Chicken Fillets (1kg)	98.50 ฿
Beef Round (1kg) (or Equivalent Back Leg Red Meat)	535.89 ฿
Apples (1kg)	80.75 ฿
Banana (1kg)	26.25 ฿
Oranges (1kg)	59.25 ฿
Tomato (1kg)	46.88 ฿
Potato (1kg)	53.33 ฿
Onion (1kg)	33.75 ฿
Lettuce (1 head)	25.00 ฿
Water (1.5 liter bottle)	14.75 ฿
Bottle of Wine (Mid-Range)	500.00 ฿
Domestic Beer (0.5 liter bottle)	56.14 ฿
Imported Beer (0.33 liter bottle)	63.67 ฿
Cigarettes 20 Pack (Marlboro)	120.00 ฿

🚗 Transportation

One-way Ticket (Local Transport)	20.00 ฿
Monthly Pass (Regular Price)	400.00 ฿
Taxi Start (Normal Tariff)	35.00 ฿
Taxi 1km (Normal Tariff)	25.00 ฿
Taxi 1hour Waiting (Normal Tariff)	150.00 ฿
Gasoline (1 liter)	42.93 ฿
Volkswagen Golf 1.4 90 KW Trendline (Or Equivalent New Car)	700,000.00 ฿
Toyota Corolla Sedan 1.6l 97kW Comfort (Or Equivalent New Car)	728,571.43 ฿

🛋 Utilities (Monthly)

Basic (Electricity, Heating, Cooling, Water, Garbage) for 85m2 Apartment	2,080.09 ฿
Mobile Phone Monthly Plan with Calls and 10GB+ Data	517.09 ฿
Internet (60 Mbps or More, Unlimited Data, Cable/ADSL)	566.00 ฿

🚴 Sports And Leisure

Fitness Club, Monthly Fee for 1 Adult	1,075.00 ฿
Tennis Court Rent (1 Hour on Weekend)	212.50 ฿
Cinema, International Release, 1 Seat	200.00 ฿

🚼 Childcare

Preschool (or Kindergarten), Full Day, Private, Monthly for 1 Child	10,750.00 ฿
International Primary School, Yearly for 1 Child	300,000.00 ฿

👕 Clothing And Shoes

1 Pair of Jeans (Levis 501 Or Similar)	630.00 ฿
1 Summer Dress in a Chain Store (Zara, H&M, ...)	1,187.50 ฿
1 Pair of Nike Running Shoes (Mid-Range)	2,000.00 ฿
1 Pair of Men Leather Business Shoes	1,791.67 ฿

🛏 Rent Per Month

Apartment (1 bedroom) in City Centre	13,500.00 ฿
Apartment (1 bedroom) Outside of Centre	8,800.00 ฿
Apartment (3 bedrooms) in City Centre	22,700.00 ฿
Apartment (3 bedrooms) Outside of Centre	22,800.00 ฿

🏢 Buy Apartment Price

Price per Square Meter to Buy Apartment in City Centre	75,714.00 ฿
Price per Square Meter to Buy Apartment Outside of Centre	31,666.67 ฿

Courtesy of www.numbeo.com

WHAT DOES HUA HIN OFFER FOR EXPATS LIVING THERE?

There doesn't seem to be much organised expat activity like in other cities of similar size in Thailand. There are the normal golf clubs that organise expat golf tournaments, lunches and dinners, tennis clubs and many bars run quiz nights for expats. There is also a newspaper that you can also access online which acts as an advertising means to advertise upcoming events, Hua Hin Today. The wonderful ladies from Chicky Net also have an online presence in Hua Hin for any retired ladies. With its close proximity to Bangkok, Hua Hin offers ex-pats the opportunity to get away for a city break and heading down south there are many beach towns within a few hours driving distance that are not so tourist-orientated and are more relaxing. One of the good things about living in Hua Hin is it is not a busy city like Bangkok and getting around is a breeze but the town is still big enough to offer everything that you seek, large shopping malls, beaches, restaurants and bars, markets and night markets, cinema, and even a couple of water parks.

PLACES TO GO AND THINGS TO DO IN HUA HIN

POPULAR BEACHES OF HUA HIN
- **Hua Hin Beach**
- **Khao Takiab Beach**
- **Khao Tao Beach**
- **Pranburi Beach**
- **Cha Am Beach**

Hua Hin and its surrounding areas have been favoured with some of the most beautiful beaches in the world. The year-round warm seas in the Gulf of Thailand have helped make the Hua Hin area a popular destination for both foreigners and Thais and is known for its clean and beautiful beaches. Though not as tropical as the beaches in Southern Thailand they are still popular with tourists, ex-pats and Bangkokians who make their way down to the coast to escape the oppressive heat of the city on weekends, and public or Buddhist holidays or whenever they can get out of the city.

HUA HIN BEACH

Hua Hin Beach is right in the centre of town and is the most popular beach in the area. When you are entering the beach from the northern end you will find a wonderful mystic Chinese Temple sitting along the walkway. Sai Nam Kheo Shrine is a small but beautiful Chinese-style temple that is built on a rocky outcrop on the shoreline which provides excellent views of the Gulf of Thailand with the wooden fish pier on one side and Hua Hin Beach on the other side of the temple. The beach stretches for over seven kilometres and all along the shore, you will find great restaurants offering visitors authentic Thai food at affordable prices. On the weekends and during Thailand's many public or Buddhist holidays, Hua Hin Beach can be quite busy. However, on weekdays, finding a secluded spot to enjoy the sand and the sun should pose no problems. If you're into water sports there are many attractions to enjoy including jet skiing, canoeing and kiteboarding. If you are not into water sports there are horseback rides that you can take along the beach.

KHAO TAKIAB BEACH

Located seven and a half kilometres drive south of Hua Hin, lies Khao Takiab Beach. If you are up to it and feel like a long walk, you can walk along the golden sands from Hua Hin Beach to Monkey Mountain at Khao Takiab but if you prefer to drive it's a nice easy 10-minute drive through the middle of town and there are plenty of parking spaces when you get there. The beach is much less developed than Hua Hin Beach, which makes it the perfect beach for people looking to experience a more relaxed setting than the more touristy Hua Hin Beach. Sitting high on top of Khao Takiab Hill, also known as Monkey Mountain is Wat Khao Lad temple which is teeming with hundreds of Macaque Monkeys, as the name Monkey Mountain suggests. The temple overlooks Khao Takiab Beach and is well worth the drive out of town to take in the wonderful temple that sits overlooking the beach.

KHAO TAO BEACH

Khao Tao Beach is a great spot to take a few hours away from the hustle and bustle of Hua Hin. The beach is in a small cove about 20 kilometres south of Hua Hin and you can walk along the stretch of beach between Khao Takiab Beach and Khao Tao Beach in about 90 minutes. Khao Tao is named for the hill that overlooks the beach and translates to Turtle Hill. At the top of this hill sits Wat Tham Khao Tao which provides some of the most beautiful views over the Gulf of Thailand with Hua Hin stretching away in the distance to the north.

PRANBURI BEACH

Pranburi is a large busy town about 30 minutes south of Hua Hin on the main highway that takes you down to Southern Thailand and as far as the Malaysian border. A few kilometres east of the main town lies the quiet Pranburi Beach. The beach stretches for miles and you can have it all to yourself as hardly any tourists come here and those that do normally stay around the swimming pools of the many hotels and resorts that are scattered along the foreshore. Weekends and evenings can get busy when the locals come here to escape the heat of Pranburi Town and on weekend evenings the road along the beach opens up as a food market with many food stalls selling Thai foods, freshly cooked seafood, BBQ pork and chicken and many other delicacies. You can then find a spot on the beach or the boardwalk to sit and enjoy the cool evening breeze from the sea.

CHA AM BEACH

About a half-hour drive north of Hua Hin you will find Cha Am Beach. If you flew into Bangkok when you arrived you would have driven through Cha Am on your drive from Bangkok Airport to Hua Hin. Cha Am Beach is a quieter version of Hua Hin Beach, though Cha Am Beach often draws large crowds on the weekends and public holidays when people come down from

Bangkok. The beach is adjacent to a picturesque tree-lined road that extends for miles in each direction. All along the road, you will find massage shops, cafes, street vendors and restaurants, many of which are known for their excellent Thai food and seafood that can be found just steps away from the beach. Most people who come to Hua Hin do so for the beaches, restaurants, bars, markets and nightlife. But there is much more to the town than those places if you take the time to look around

KHAO HIN LEK FAI LOOKOUT
A 2-kilometre drive out of town up Soi 88 you will find Hin Lek Fey Lookout which rises 160 meters above sea level with stunning views over Hua Hin that stretch towards Cha Am to the north and as far south as Khao Takiab. If you're an early riser it would be a good idea to visit early in the morning when the sun rises over the horizon as it's a stunning view and a great photo opportunity. Many wild monkeys live on the mountain.

HUTSADIN ELEPHANT FOUNDATION
Personally, I don't like or frequent any live animal shows such as Elephant shows, Monkey shows or Snake shows that are found all over Thailand, but I often visit and donate to animal sanctuaries. Hutsadin Elephant Foundation is a Hua Hin elephant rescue organization, with the aim of rescuing elephants abandoned by their owners due to ill health, old age or simply because they are unable to work any longer and are too expensive to feed. The foundation is a non-profit organisation and any funds received directly benefit the elephants. Here you can have close contact and mingle with the elephants in their natural habitat. The sanctuary is about a ten-minute drive west of downtown Hua Hin.

RAJABHAKTI PARK
Rajabhakti Park with its towering statues of seven of the Great Kings of Thailand, was officially opened by the then Crown Prince Maha Vajiralongkorn, now His Majesty King

Rama X in 2015. The Park is one of Hua Hin's most significant attractions but more so for Thai people who worship their kings both past and present it was built as a place to come and pay respect to Thai royalty. The seven Kings are: King Ram Khamhaeng (1279-1298), King Naresuan (1590-1605), King Narai (1656-1688), King Taksin (1767-1782), King Rama I (1782-1809), King Mongkut (1851-1868), King Chulalongkorn (1868-1910). The park's peripheral area is a huge 201,600 square meters consisting of the surrounding landscape and support facilities displaying information about each of the Great Kings.

You will find Rajabhakti Park on the main highway out of town about a ten-minute drive south.

WAT HUAY MONGKOL

Wat Huay Mongkol is a temple dedicated to the famous Thai monk Luang Phor Thuad who lived to be 100 years old from 1582 to 1682 and is located on the western outskirts of Hua Hin. The monk is shrouded in many stories and mythology about the miracles that he performed, one of which was converting seawater into fresh water on a sea voyage when the ship that he was sailing in ran out of fresh drinking water, which is the Buddhist equivalent of Jesus turning water into wine. The temple incorporates a massive statue of Luang Phor Thuad who sits on a mound that is accessed by a set of stairs. There you will find many Thai people making merit and praying for help in their lives The impressive statue of the monk is about 12 meters tall and 10 meters wide. The temple is very popular with Thai people who come from all over the country to pay respect to Luang Phor Thuad and to ask for favour, good luck, health, fortune and happiness. Back down the steps and below the statue, there are huge three-headed wooden elephants where Buddhist devotees walk in circles three times under the belly of the elephants as they believe that walking under the elephants brings good fortune, so there is always a huge crowd circling under the elephant structure. The complex also holds a

Buddhist temple, a statue of King Taksin the Great on horseback and shops where Buddhist amulets and artefacts can be bought. After coming back down from the statue of Luang Phor Thud take a walk down to the lake that is teeming with huge fish and turtles. You can buy fish food for a few baht and feed the fish as this is also supposed to bring you good luck.

MONSOON VALLEY VINEYARD
The Monsoon Valley Vineyard is nestled in a beautiful valley and is the home to Monsoon Valley Wines and is about a 45-minute drive west of downtown Hua Hin. Visitors can enjoy a wine tasting of the new latitude wines and tour the vineyard by jeep or elephant. The Sala Restaurant, Wine Bar & Bistro is also open on the property for meals and drinks.

BLACK MOUNTAIN WATER PARK
Black Mountain Water Park is a sprawling water park about a 20-minute drive from the centre of Hua Hin and is close to the elephant sanctuary so you could visit both attractions on the same day. The park comprises nine water slides, a kid's pool, a wave pool, and the lazy river along with its own golf course. It is situated close to the Black Mountain Cable-Ski Lake, an artificial lake if cable skiing is your thing.

MRIGADAYAVAN PALACE
Located in between Hua Hin and Cha-am the Mrigadayavan Palace is the former summer residence of King Vajiravudh or King Rama VI of Thailand, and was commissioned by His Majesty to serve as his seaside residence during the latter years of his reign. The monarch's personal physician had recommended he spend more time by the ocean so that his rheumatoid arthritis could be eased by its warm air and abundant breezes. The palace was built raised from the ground on pillars and made entirely from recycled teak wood. The Summer Palace's very attractive architectural style is completely different from that of the other Thai palaces. After the King died

in 1925, the palace was left deserted for many years. Today, it has been fully restored and you can still see some of the King's furniture such as his writing desk with pencils and paper, sofa and his bed. Walking around the palace will give you a rare insight into how the Thai Royal Family used to live almost a century ago. After visiting the palace, you can enjoy a walk on the nature trail in the surrounding mangrove forest.

PA LA-U WATERFALL

Kaeng Krachan National Park extends 2914 km² from the South from Prachuap Khiri Khan Province to the north with Petchaburi Province and hugging the Myanmar border on the western side. The National Park is a protected rainforest that holds diverse wildlife such as leopards, elephants and gibbons just to mention a few. There are also Tigers but as in the rest of the world, they are not as common as before. Within the national park is the Pa La-U Waterfall. It's a bit of a drive to get there (about a ninety-minute drive north-west of Hua Hin) but it is well worth the effort especially during or just after the wet season when the waterfall is flowing to full capacity. The Road leading to Pa La-U Waterfall is stunning, as the road winds over the Kaeng Krachan National Park Mountains. The Pal La-U Waterfall has five levels that are open to the public, the first two levels are easy to reach but the climb gets harder as you progress up the mountain, so good walking shoes are a necessity.

WHAT TO DO WHEN THE SUN GOES DOWN IN HUA HI?

HUA HIN NIGHT MARKET

Hua Hin has many night markets but the one most frequented by tourists is the Hua Hin Night Market in the centre of town, off Patchkasem Road. By day the market is a normal street but at night time the area is closed to traffic and comes alive after 6.00 pm with brightly lit-up stalls when traders line the street selling arts and crafts, clothing, souvenirs and of course street food. At the western end of the market, there are stalls set up outside of the many restaurants selling freshly caught seafood. Everything from whole fish to huge lobsters and prawns. You make your selection and they weigh it and you pay for it by the gram then you go inside the restaurant while they cook it to your liking and then serve it to you inside the restaurant. There are also a few bars along the street where you can sit for a pre-dinner drink or after dinner and listen to live music. Just around the corner is a local market, Chat Chai Market that is open in the daytime and is frequented by local Thais. They sell every kind of food that you can think of but at a lot cheaper price than the night market because the market is geared towards the locals.

CICADA MARKET

Cicada Market is a night market that combines contemporary arts and crafts, home decorations and clothes both new and second-hand with a large variety of food outlets. The Market is divided into four zones. The first zone is shopping, the second zone is the Amphitheatre, a semicircle outdoor stage for live performances, the third zone is the art section, and the fourth zone is the food area where you can get freshly cooked food from various regions of Thailand such as Spicy Green Papaya Salad, Tom Yum Goong, Moo Laab, Khao Pad, Thai red and green curries, Pad Thai, Tom Kha Gai and spicy BBQ chicken, there is also a wide choice of fresh seafood cooked to order and some Western food stalls. The market is a little way out of town on the road that leads to Khao Takiab.

TAMARIND MARKET

Tamarind Market sits right next door to Cicada Market so it is possible to enjoy both markets on the same night. The night market comes alive every Thursday, Friday, Saturday and Sunday night and has an open stage where live music performances take place. There is a huge selection of foods from many countries including Chinese, Malay, Indian and of course, Thai and there are also plenty of Western food outlets selling pizza, BBQ Pork Ribs, Bratwurst sausage and fried and

BBQ chicken. Unlike Cicada Market, Tamarind Market only has food stalls and not clothing or arts and crafts stalls.

BAAN KHUN POR

Probably my favourite place to hang out in Hua Hin on an evening is the well-renowned Baan Khun Por. Ban Khun Por translates to My Father's House and it is a huge outdoor entertainment and food complex complete with many food outlets selling both Thai and Western foods which many expats and Thais frequent. They have live music on the huge stage seven nights a week and sometimes they have Thai music superstars performing and the whole complex is packed to the rafters. Apart from the great music scene, the other reason that the venue is so popular is its prices. A large Chang Beer is only 65 baht which is a similar price that you would pay in a 7-11 store to take home and drink and you can buy most meals for under 100 baht which not only makes it a fun night out but also a cheap night out.

ROCK ZONE

The Rock Zone is probably the best live rock music bar in Hua Hin. They have different bands playing seven nights a week and they play mainly western rock music. Everything from Led Zeppelin to Deep Purple from Jimmy Hendrix to Guns and Roses The live music normally starts around 9.00 pm and goes on into the night. Tam is the owner and he started playing the drums when he was just a kid he still sits in and jams with the bands most nights and now his son Namo who is around 5 years old occasionally jams with the band also and he is a spectacular drummer.

SOI BINTABAHT

There are three main lady bar areas in Hua Hin. Bintabaht which is right in the middle of the tourist area in downtown Hua Hin and just opposite the Hilton Hotel which used to be the busiest lady bar area in Hua Hin but since COVID raised its ugly head and tourism declined in Thailand it has lost its crown to Soi 94. Now walking down Soi Bintabaht you will find many bars have closed their doors. So, if lady bars are your thing, I suggest you visit Soi 94.

SOI 94

Soi 94 is now the busiest and most frequented bar area in Hua Hin. The soi is over the western side of the main railway track that dissects the town and it goes around in a massive square. The busiest complex is Wonderland which sits opposite the 7-11 corner store close to the railway crossing but a new area has just been built on the side street that Rock Zone sits on. There are more bars in the Soi 94 area, behind Baan Khun Por and also opposite Le Pub further west.

SOI 80

Soi 80 is another bar area that has taken a bit of a downturn since COVID-19. The street lies just off Sukhumvit Road right in the middle of town and the whole street is teaming with bars with beautiful girls and some not so beautiful, sitting at the front of the bars touting for your business.

THE FOOD IN HUA HIN

There is no doubt that there are some fantastic restaurants in Hua Hin. For seafood, you can't go past Saeng Thai Seafood, a very popular restaurant near the fishing pier. Your meal comes with an amazing view of the coastline, and the seafood is caught fresh daily by local fishermen. There is also a seafood market in Khao Takiab, about a 15-minute drive south of Hua Hin Beach next to where the fishing boats come in. Here you can get seafood that came fresh from the sea that morning cooked to order in one of the many restaurants along the street.

Many restaurants in Hua Hin cater for Western tastes, Italian pizza and pasta, German, Australian, USA, and many that cater for English food, including Le Pub which serves a fantastic Sunday Roast and Friday Fish n Chips, and Cheers Bar is run by an Australian but does both Thai and English food and other Western fare.

HUA HIN HOSPITALS AND MEDICAL FACILITIES

There are seven hospitals in Hua Hin the largest being the government Hua Hin Hospital. This hospital has an entire floor dedicated to the Thai Royal Family. This government-run hospital is used mainly by the local Thai population, and therefore treatment is quite inexpensive but obviously gets crowded. Most of the hospital offers twenty-four-hour accident and emergency departments and medical services including general surgery, neurology, orthopaedics and cardiology, and neurology. Hua Hin has many dental clinics that provide a full range of dental services at a price range substantially lower than in Western countries, and also lower compared to Phuket, Bangkok and Pattaya.

Hospitals in Hua Hin include:
Bangkok Hospital Hua Hin
San Paolo Hospital
Hua Hin International Polyclinic

Red Cross Hospital

THE DOWNSIDES OF LIVING IN HUA HIN.

THE TOWN GETS VERY BUSY AT WEEKENDS AND BUDDHIST HOLIDAYS

One of the good things about living in Hua Hin is its proximity to Bangkok should you want a city break or if you are returning to your own country for a holiday and you are flying out of Bangkok. The problem is, that that can also have a downside, as on weekends, public holidays and Buddhist holidays hordes of Bangkokians head to Hua Hin to escape the overbearing heat and the air pollution that tends to engulf the city.

THE BEACHES ARE NOT SO TROPICAL AS FURTHER DOWN SOUTH

Hua Hin has some lovely beaches that stretch down from Cha-Am in the north through Hua Hin and then on to Khao Takiab and Khao Tao in the south. However, they are not as tropical as the beaches a few hundred kilometres further south of the town. They are still beautiful but the waters are rarely crystal clear like the beach towns and islands such as Koh Samui, Koh Phangan and Krabi and they lack the palm trees that go hand in hand with tropical beaches. Hua Hin Beach in the centre of town also has many rocks that are encrusted with shells that when the tide is out and they are hidden can cut your feet badly. As you walk further south towards Khao Takiab they disappear so if you like swimming in the sea it is better to find a beach a little way out of town.

KRABI

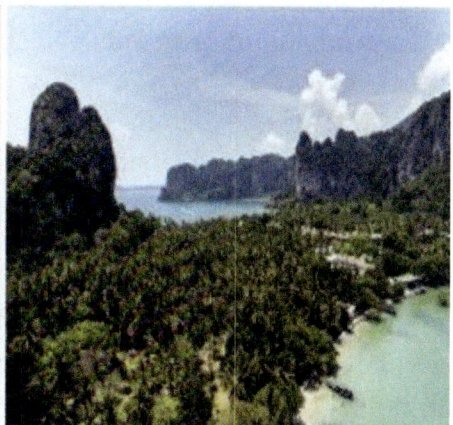

CHAPTER SIX

KRABI

Krabi is fast becoming a favourite place for ex-pats to retire. With its relaxed laid-back feel, Krabi brings to mind how Phuket was when I first came to Thailand all those years ago in 1983. Krabi has a very low crime rate and is often recognized as one of the safest places to live in the country. Located on the west coast with a low crime rate, and palm-fringed beaches. Krabi is an ideal destination and well worth a look before deciding where to live or retire in Thailand. The Krabi area is naturally blessed with tropical beaches, and with the backdrop of the many limestone cliffs Krabi is a photographer's dream

Krabi Town is a busy metropolitan area and the hub of the banking and business sectors of the district. Most ex-pats live in the beach areas of Krabi with the most popular being Ao Nang and Nopparatthara Beach both about a thirty-minute drive south of Krabi Town. Krabi is also the focal point for ferries to many of the beautiful Islands in Thailand. Ferries depart regularly to Phi-Phi Island, Koh Lanta and Phuket from Klong Jilad Pier. Krabi is also a melting pot for different cultures and religions. There is a large Muslim presence and also a smaller Indian presence here which makes it a great place to be for finding different foods from different countries. There are two golf courses in Krabi, the 18-hole Pakasai Country Club, located 40km south of Krabi Town. There is also a 9-hole course in Klong Muang, at the Sofitel Phokeethra Resort, which is also open to non-residents of the hotel

FACTS ABOUT KRABI

- Krabi Town and its beach areas Population: 33,000
- Krabi Province population: 470,000
- Krabi has a tropical savanna climate. with average temperatures of 24°C to 32°C all year-round. The wettest months are generally September and

October.

- Krabi lies approximately 800 kilometres south of Bangkok
- Krabi Town is the capital of southern Thailand's Krabi Province. The main tourist area is about a twenty-minute drive south of town with Ao Nang being the most popular beach town in Krabi Province.
- Krabi province is composed of over 150 small islands that are dispersed along the southwest coast of Thailand. Among these islands, Koh Phi-Phi, Koh Lanta, and Koh Jum are the most popular.
- Ao Nang Beach, extending up to 20 kilometres, is reputed to be one of the longest beaches in Thailand
- Though you will see many images and sculptures of crabs in the area, Krabi means sword, not crab
- Krabi has a large Indian population more so in the tourist beach towns where people of Indian descent own many businesses
- Krabi has a large Muslim population compared to central and northern Thailand around 34% and the Islamic domes of the mystic mosques are a common site in Krabi and Southern Thailand.

KRABI'S WEATHER
Krabi's weather is similar to Phuket with the same wet season from May to October.

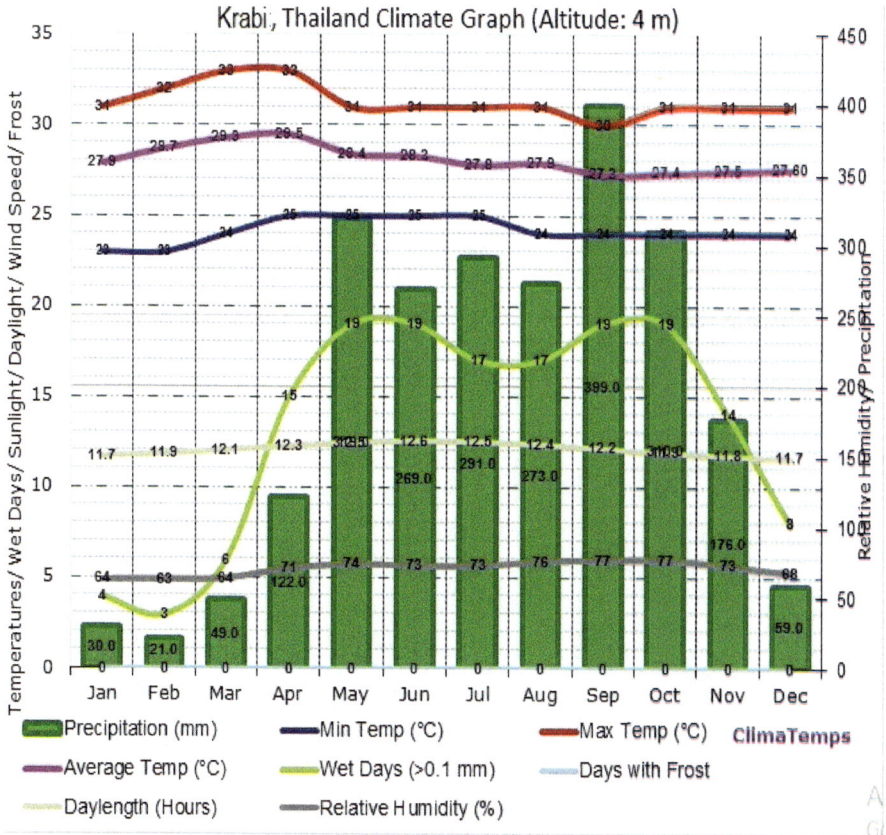

Courtesy of www.travelfish.org.com

THE COST OF LIVING IN KRABI

Krabi for some reason that I can't understand can be a little more expensive to live in than other tourist towns, especially the main tourist areas like Ao Nang and Nopparatthara Beach. But if you get away from those areas it's a lot less expensive to live in and you will find cheaper accommodation and food outlets.

Rent Prices in Krabi are 40.7% lower than in Bangkok

Restaurant Prices in Krabi are 19.4% lower than in Bangkok

Groceries Prices in Krabi are 4.7% lower than in Bangkok

🍴 Restaurants

Meal, Inexpensive Restaurant	50.00 ฿
Meal for 2 People, Mid-range Restaurant, Three-course	750.00 ฿
McMeal at McDonalds (or Equivalent Combo Meal)	190.00 ฿
Domestic Beer (0.5 liter draught)	90.00 ฿
Imported Beer (0.33 liter bottle)	100.00 ฿
Cappuccino (regular)	85.67 ฿
Coke/Pepsi (0.33 liter bottle)	25.33 ฿
Water (0.33 liter bottle)	12.50 ฿

🛒 Markets

Milk (regular), (1 liter)	63.33 ฿
Loaf of Fresh White Bread (500g)	75.67 ฿
Rice (white), (1kg)	67.50 ฿
Eggs (regular) (12)	81.60 ฿
Local Cheese (1kg)	916.67 ฿
Chicken Fillets (1kg)	100.00 ฿
Beef Round (1kg) (or Equivalent Back Leg Red Meat)	283.33 ฿
Apples (1kg)	79.00 ฿
Banana (1kg)	30.00 ฿
Oranges (1kg)	70.00 ฿
Tomato (1kg)	57.50 ฿
Potato (1kg)	42.50 ฿
Onion (1kg)	42.50 ฿
Lettuce (1 head)	64.50 ฿
Water (1.5 liter bottle)	22.50 ฿
Bottle of Wine (Mid-Range)	400.00 ฿
Domestic Beer (0.5 liter bottle)	55.00 ฿
Imported Beer (0.33 liter bottle)	80.00 ฿
Cigarettes 20 Pack (Marlboro)	70.00 ฿

🚐 Transportation

One-way Ticket (Local Transport)	20.00 ฿
Monthly Pass (Regular Price)	?
Taxi Start (Normal Tariff)	?
Taxi 1km (Normal Tariff)	20.00 ฿
Taxi 1hour Waiting (Normal Tariff)	200.00 ฿
Gasoline (1 liter)	39.98 ฿
Volkswagen Golf 1.4 90 KW Trendline (Or Equivalent New Car)	600,000.00 ฿
Toyota Corolla Sedan 1.6l 97kW Comfort (Or Equivalent New Car)	850,000.00 ฿

🛋 Utilities (Monthly)

Basic (Electricity, Heating, Cooling, Water, Garbage) for 85m2 Apartment	1,500.00 ฿
Mobile Phone Monthly Plan with Calls and 10GB+ Data	500.00 ฿
Internet (60 Mbps or More, Unlimited Data, Cable/ADSL)	600.00 ฿

🚲 Sports And Leisure

Fitness Club, Monthly Fee for 1 Adult	1,250.00 ฿
Tennis Court Rent (1 Hour on Weekend)	?
Cinema, International Release, 1 Seat	200.00 ฿

🛒 Childcare

Preschool (or Kindergarten), Full Day, Private, Monthly for 1 Child	18,500.00 ฿
International Primary School, Yearly for 1 Child	300,000.00 ฿

👕 Clothing And Shoes

1 Pair of Jeans (Levis 501 Or Similar)	1,400.00 ฿
1 Summer Dress in a Chain Store (Zara, H&M, ...)	800.00 ฿
1 Pair of Nike Running Shoes (Mid-Range)	2,750.00 ฿
1 Pair of Men Leather Business Shoes	1,200.00 ฿

🛏 Rent Per Month

Apartment (1 bedroom) in City Centre	18,500.00 ฿
Apartment (1 bedroom) Outside of Centre	13,333.33 ฿
Apartment (3 bedrooms) in City Centre	23,333.33 ฿
Apartment (3 bedrooms) Outside of Centre	18,000.00 ฿

🏢 Buy Apartment Price

Price per Square Meter to Buy Apartment in City Centre	?
Price per Square Meter to Buy Apartment Outside of Centre	?

Courtesy of www.numbio.com

WHAT DOES KRABI OFFER FOR EXPATS LIVING THERE?

It has been estimated that there are around three thousand expats living in the Krabi area, including the neighbouring island of Koh Lanta. That's not a lot, mainly because it's only recently been discovered as an ex-pat and retiree destination. Another reason is that it is a long way to places like Hua Hin, Bangkok, Pattaya and the northern cities like Chiang Mai, Khon Kaen, Korat and Udon Thani should you want to travel around Thailand as many ex-pat retirees living in Thailand like to do. There is not much in the way of organised meetings or outings. As far as my research has gone, I have been unable to find any expat clubs or associations. Krabi is small compared to other towns that retirees and ex-pats are drawn to. I believe this will change in the future as more and more retirees discover the benefits of living in Krabi. After a while of living here, you start to recognise people by sight and their accents. There are quite a few bars and restaurants in Ao Nang and Krabi Town where expats tend to gather. If you're British look out for the bars advertising Premier League football and if you are Australian look out for them advertising Aussie Rules and so on, as that's where you will find some of your fellow compatriots.

***See Useful Website pages at the end of
this book for expat club links**

PLACES TO GO AND THINGS TO DO IN KRABI

POPULAR BEACHES OF KRABI
- **Ao Nang**
- **Railay Beach**
- **Noppharat Thara Beach**
- **Tonsai Beach**
- **Phra Nang Beach**

- **Tub Kaek Beach**
- **Klong Muang Beach**

AO NANG BEACH

Ao Nang Beach runs about a kilometre along the town's promenade, and with Krabi being on the east side of Thailand so you will be able to view Thailand's world-famous sunsets from Ao Nang Beach. All along the street that runs parallel to the beach, you will find lined with restaurants, bars and souvenir shops. At the northern end of the street, you will find the longboats that will take you around to the world-famous Railay Beach.

RAILAY BEACH

Railay Beach is the jewel in the crown of Krabi. Once a quiet fishing village, Railay Beach is now a bustling beach town with many luxury resorts restaurants and bars. It is accessible only by longboat from Ao Nang Pier or from Krabi town and should not be missed. The beach is about a thirty-minute boat ride around the bay passing close to the limestone cliffs that surround the peninsular. When you get to your destination you will be rewarded with a stunning long golden beach with more limestone cliffs as a backdrop to the beach which you can climb to get magnificent views across the Andaman Sea.

NOPPHARAT THARA BEACH

Noppharat Thara Beach is just a short walk from the centre of Ao Nang. There are many great restaurants here and most are a lot cheaper than in downtown Ao Nang.

TONSAI BEACH

Tonsai Beach lies between Ao Nang Beach and Railay Beach. With soaring cliffs towering above the shoreline. Tonsai Beach might be small, but it features several trendy bars where you can enjoy a cold drink and take in the sunset.

PHRA NANG BEACH

Phra Nang Beach is one of the most stunning beach areas along the Krabi coast, with its long golden sandy beach overlooking the Andaman Sea. Here you will also find Phra Nang Cave, also known as The Princess Cave and within the cave is a shrine that is dedicated to health and fertility.

TUB KAEK BEACH
Tub Kaek Beach is a great destination for travellers looking for a quiet spot away from the maddening crowds. Set along Krabi's western coast, this tranquil location is just a 30-minute drive from Ao Nang. The white sandy beach offers stunning views of the many distant surrounding limestone islands.

KLONG MUANG BEACH
Lying about 15 kilometres from Ao Nang is Klong Muang Beach. If you want to escape from the busy beach areas that lie closer to town such as Ao Nang and Railay this short drive will bring you to this serene location where you can have the beach virtually all to yourself.

Ao Nang Beach is by far the most popular place to live in Krabi Province and a fantastic place to visit but I have to say that it can be a little bit more expensive to stay here than in many other places in Thailand especially if you stick to the main walking street that runs the length of the beach. I have always found when visiting Krabi that the further from town you get and the less popular the beach towns are with tourists the cheaper it gets. Ao Nang can also be annoying in some respects because the tourist outlets and business owners in the downtown area can be quite aggressive in trying to get you to spend your hard-earned money in their shops, bars or restaurants. Having said that it's still a great area of Thailand to live if you want a more laid-back lifestyle. Krabi is a melting pot of different ethnicities, religions and cultures which is great for any tourist visiting a country and why it's on the tourist's radar. The different cuisines from southern, central and northern Thailand go hand in hand with Hallal Muslim, Indian, Chinese and Malaysian cuisines. If you're into temples and religious architecture then you are in for a treat as not only are there many unique Buddhist Temples surrounding the area but there are also many Islamic Mosques and while walking around the area you can hear the mournful cries to summon Muslims to prayer from the minaret several times a day.

WAT THAM SEUA (TIGER CAVE)

The Tiger Cave Temple, also known as Wat Tham Suea, is one of the most revered and sacred Buddhist temples in Thailand and is famous for the tiger paw prints that are found within the cave. The history of the Tiger Cave temple in Krabi dates back to 1975 when a Vipassana monk named Ajahn Jumnean entered the cave to meditate. During his meditation, he witnessed tigers roaming around the cave and this discovery led to the building and naming of the temple, Wat Tham Suea, or Tiger Cave. Here it gets confusing as another legend says that an actual huge tiger used to live and roam the cave and the naming of the temple comes from discoveries of tiger paw prints on the cave walls, also the cave is shaped like a tiger's paw. To get to the top of the mountain to see the temple in all its glory is not for the faint-hearted as it's a challenging 1260 steps to get to the top.

THE MONKEY TRAIL CLIFF WALK TO PAI PLONG BEACH

A fun way to spend a few hours is to take the winding path through the rainforest from the end of Ao Nang Beach to Pai Plong Beach. Pai Plong Beach is only accessible by taking a hike through the jungle or by boat. It is called The Monkey Trail Cliff Walk but in all of the years I have been coming here I have never seen a monkey on the trail but some people tell me that they have so you may be lucky and see some but if not, the walk is lovely and the beach at the other end is sensational.

MOUNTAIN VIEW RESTAURANT

About a ten-minute drive along the main road from Ao Nang,

you will find the Mountain View Restaurant which sits in the middle of a rain forest and is built into the side of one of the limestone cliffs. With a great atmosphere delicious Thai food and an interesting menu it's a beautiful rustic restaurant during the day but at night turns into a bar with great food and live music.

WHAT TO DO WHEN THE SUN GOES DOWN IN KRABI

KRABI TOWN NIGHT MARKET

Krabi Town is the capital of the province of Krabi and the main commercial and transport hub for the area. Although Krabi Town isn't as great a tourist destination as the beach areas such as Ao Nang and Railay it is still worth a visit. On the Manutboraan intersection on Maharat Road not far from the riverfront and within the main shopping zone of the town. every Friday, Saturday and Sunday night between 4.00 pm and 10.00 pm, you will find the Krabi Weekend Night Market when the area closes to traffic and transforms into a walking street market with over 70 food vendors and stalls selling clothes, accessories arts and crafts and many other things. On the stage in the middle of Walking Street, they have live music performers throughout the night and you can choose what food to eat, buy a drink and sit and listen to some great Thai music performers.

AO NANG BEACH LANDMARK NIGHT MARKET

Ao Nang restaurants are a lot more expensive than in most tourist towns in Thailand for some mysterious reason that I have never found the answer to. So, if you are on a budget or if like me you don't like to waste your hard-earned money to make someone else richer you will be happy to know the beach town has a night market, Ao Nang Landmark Night Market, that is located next to Noppharat Thara Beach and close to the Muay Thai stadium. There is also a smaller night market in Ao Nang just a little way from the beach on the road that leads to Krabi Town. As well as selling great food from around Asia at a great price they also sell clothing, jewellery, arts and crafts and souvenirs. The Ao Nang Landmark Night Market is at Noppharat Thara Beach, directly adjacent to KFC.

THE HILLTOP RESTAURANT

The Hilltop is without a doubt Ao Nang's most stylish restaurant and the go-to place for locals and tourists. The restaurant is known for its authentic Thai cuisine but it's the breathtaking views of the sunset that sets it apart from all the other restaurants in Ao Nang. The outdoor seating area provides panoramic views over the coastal waters during the day and the sunset when the sun is going down and is an experience not to be missed. If that's not enough they also have live music in the evening. Make sure that you make a reservation as with the food and views being exceptional the tables fill up fast.

BARS AND LADY BAR

Ao Nang has an exciting nightlife scene. And there is no shortage of lady bars or even ladyboy bars if that's your thing as the Blue Dragon Cabaret Bar has a well-known Lady Boy show. The bar is located along Ao Nang's Beach Road close to the RCA Complex. The RCA Entertainment Venue is Ao Nang's premier nightlife scene and you will find it right in the middle of town, opposite the beach on the Beach Road. The bar complex has over twenty bars filled with beautiful young ladies, and some not so young or beautiful, vying for your custom. There are many more lady bars scattered throughout Ao Nang and also many normal bars with live music playing into the early hours of the morning in many of them. If you just want to relax and have a few drinks and not buy any lady drinks then another popular bar area in Ao Nang is Center Point which has about a dozen bars within its complex. If you want to kick up your heels there are two nightclubs in Ao Nang Moonshine and Sabina. Noppharat Thara Beach and Pai Plong Beach two of the neighbouring beach areas close to Ao Nang have many good restaurants and a few bars as well, but Ao Nang is where most of the action is.

The Last Fisherman Bar

One of the most popular beachside bars in Ao Nang is The Last Fisherman Bar and after The Hilltop Restaurant this is my preferred spot for sunset drinks or a beachside meal. The Last Fisherman's Bar sits directly on the beach and is just a short walk down from where the Beach Road turns up the hill to go out of town. Here you can sit at dusk and watch the longtail boats ferry their passengers back from Railay Beach while sipping on a very reasonably priced cocktail. At the Hilltop Restaurant, you will pay much more for food and drinks than you do at The Last Fisherman

EATING OUT IN KRABI

There are some absolutely wonderful places to eat in Krabi. The beach town of Ao Nang is the busiest area after Krabi Town with everything from roadside stalls to 5-star dining. Walk along the beachfront street and find lots of little restaurants offering cheap food and drinks to try to entice you inside.

There is a small Indian community in Krabi so if you like Indian food, you won't be disappointed. Drive up the hill to the Hilltop Restaurant for amazing international and Thai food, with views from the mountains to the sea. If you walk back down the hill, turn left and continue walking past The Golden Beach Resort for about five hundred meters, you will find The Last Fisherman Bar, it's a lovely spot to watch the sun go down with a cool drink and finger food. Just a short longboat ride around the bay and the limestone cliffs, you will find the hidden gem of Railay Beach, which is only accessible by long boat and is a great place to go for the day and stay for lunch or dinner.

KRABI'S HOSPITALS AND MEDICAL FACILITIES
There are three hospitals in Krabi two public and one private.
Krabi Town and Ao Nang also have medical clinics.
The hospitals of Krabi are.
Nakharin International Hospital (the newest and best hospital)
Krabi Municipal hospital
Ruam Paet Hospital (A Muslim run private hospital)

THE DOWNSIDES OF LIVING IN KRABI.

THE LONG DISTANCE FROM EVERYWHERE ELSE IN THAILAND:

As in Phuket and Koh Samui If you are considering living in Krabi with the idea of regular travel around Thailand then you may find that it is quite remote and restrictive when it comes to going to other areas of the country. Krabi is a ten-hour drive to Bangkok, Pattaya is a twelve-hour drive and Chiang Mai is a twenty-hour drive so you may find that you are limited if you want to see more of Thailand. On the plus side, the Malaysian border at Perlis is just a five-hour drive south, Phuket is a three-hour drive or two hours if you take the ferry and Koh Samui is a two-and-a-half-hour drive plus a two-hour ferry across the Gulf of Thailand. The beautiful Phi-Phi Island is just a short ferry ride away.

MORE EXPENSIVE THAN OTHER AREAS IN THAILAND

As with Phuket, I have found Krabi to be more expensive to live in than most other places in Thailand. Having an international airport Krabi gets its fair share of tourists which is guaranteed to push up the prices. Similar to Phuket and Koh Samui, Krabi is situated a long distance from Bangkok which means that getting produce to Krabi from Bangkok is expensive. The costs are then passed on to the consumer so it is more expensive to live there than in places that are closer to Bangkok such as Hua Hin. The higher costs are not so noticeable for tourists as the prices are still a lot lower than in their own countries and they only stay a few weeks but if you are planning on living in Krabi permanently your money won't stretch as far as it would in many other areas in Thailand.

CHIANG RAI

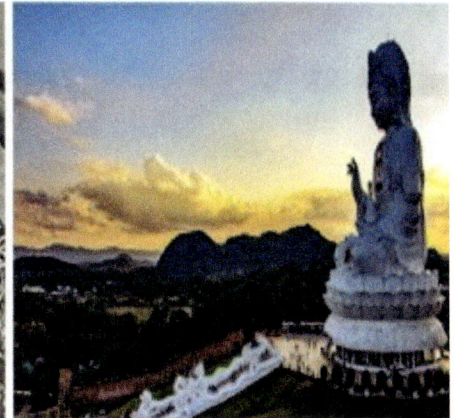

CHAPTER SEVEN

CHIANG RAI

If you're on a tight budget and need to make your pension stretch, you can't go past Chiang Rai. The city is located about two hundred kilometres northeast of Chiang Mai, close to both the Laos and Myanmar borders It's a beautiful though somewhat remote city and is surrounded by mountains, rice fields, and stunning waterfalls. It won't suit everyone; you would need to be happy in a more rural setting to live here. The people are the same friendly faces you see in Chiang Mai and it's one of the cheapest places to live in Thailand. There are four golf courses in the area. Chiang Rai has an International Airport and a bus service to Chiang Mai every hour. The journey takes between three and three and half hours depending on the schedule. Chiang Rai also has the same problem with farmers burning their fields creating air pollution so keep that in mind if you have respiratory or medical problems. Whatever town you decide to retire in, always stay for at least six months, and if it suits you make a more permanent commitment.

FACTS ABOUT CHIANG RAI

- Population: Chiang Rai City has a population of around 200,00
- Chiang Rai has a tropical savanna climate similar to its close neighbour Chiang Mai with warm to hot weather year-round, though nighttime conditions during the dry season can be cool and much lower than the

daytime highs.
- Chiang Rai lies 800 kilometres north of Bangkok
- Chiang Rai Province has a population of 1.2 million
- Chiang Rai is the capital of the Province of Chiang Rai
- Chiang Rai is the most northern border city in Thailand.
- Chiang Rai City is close to both the borders of Laos and Myanmar
- Chiang Rai is synonymous with The Golden Triangle, famous for its rich production of opium and is located in the border areas of Thailand, Myanmar, and Laos.

THE CHIANG RAI WEATHER

In Chiang Rai, the weather is similar to that of Chiang Mai. The Hot Season is from March through May. Daytime temperatures can be very hot during this period. The rainy Season is from May through October and the cool Season is from November through February.

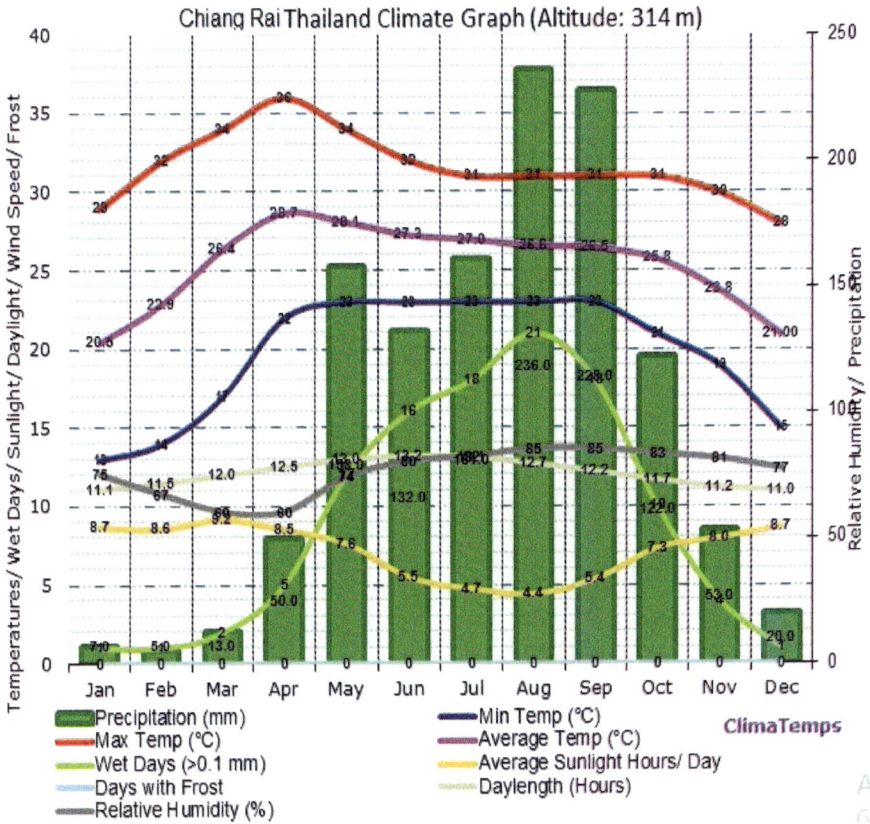

Courtesy of www.travelfish.com

THE CHIANG RAI COST OF LIVING

Consumer Prices in Chiang Rai are 30.9% lower than in Bangkok (without rent)

Consumer Prices Including Rent in Chiang Rai are 38.0% lower than in Bangkok

Rent Prices in Chiang Rai are 56.3% lower than in Bangkok

Restaurant Prices in Chiang Rai are 35.6% lower than in Bangkok

Groceries Prices in Chiang Rai are 25.0% lower than in Bangkok

Local Purchasing Power in Chiang Rai is 19.7% lower than in Bangkok

It doesn't get much cheaper to live than living in Chiang Rai. You can live a very nice lifestyle for a fraction of what it costs back in your home country. Your pension will go much further here and hopefully allow you to live in comfort and you will be able to travel the rest of Thailand and South East Asia with what you save.

✗ Restaurants

Meal, Inexpensive Restaurant	50.00 ฿
Meal for 2 People, Mid-range Restaurant, Three-course	500.00 ฿
McMeal at McDonalds (or Equivalent Combo Meal)	200.00 ฿
Domestic Beer (0.5 liter draught)	60.00 ฿
Imported Beer (0.33 liter bottle)	120.00 ฿
Cappuccino (regular)	53.75 ฿
Coke/Pepsi (0.33 liter bottle)	17.50 ฿
Water (0.33 liter bottle)	10.50 ฿

🛒 Markets

Milk (regular), (1 liter)	54.47 ฿
Loaf of Fresh White Bread (500g)	44.53 ฿
Rice (white), (1kg)	31.67 ฿
Eggs (regular) (12)	55.33 ฿
Local Cheese (1kg)	487.50 ฿
Chicken Fillets (1kg)	79.27 ฿
Beef Round (1kg) (or Equivalent Back Leg Red Meat)	375.00 ฿
Apples (1kg)	78.33 ฿
Banana (1kg)	31.67 ฿
Oranges (1kg)	41.67 ฿
Tomato (1kg)	23.33 ฿
Potato (1kg)	45.00 ฿
Onion (1kg)	30.00 ฿
Lettuce (1 head)	30.00 ฿
Water (1.5 liter bottle)	13.67 ฿
Bottle of Wine (Mid-Range)	450.00 ฿
Domestic Beer (0.5 liter bottle)	62.17 ฿
Imported Beer (0.33 liter bottle)	100.00 ฿
Cigarettes 20 Pack (Marlboro)	120.00 ฿

🚗 Transportation

One-way Ticket (Local Transport)	25.00 ฿
Monthly Pass (Regular Price)	1,000.00 ฿
Taxi Start (Normal Tariff)	40.00 ฿
Taxi 1km (Normal Tariff)	45.00 ฿
Taxi 1hour Waiting (Normal Tariff)	100.00 ฿
Gasoline (1 liter)	41.25 ฿
Volkswagen Golf 1.4 90 KW Trendline (Or Equivalent New Car)	630,000.00 ฿
Toyota Corolla Sedan 1.6l 97kW Comfort (Or Equivalent New Car)	801,666.67 ฿

🗄 Utilities (Monthly)

Basic (Electricity, Heating, Cooling, Water, Garbage) for 85m2 Apartment	1,550.00 ฿
Mobile Phone Monthly Plan with Calls and 10GB+ Data	477.55 ฿
Internet (60 Mbps or More, Unlimited Data, Cable/ADSL)	483.17 ฿

🚲 Sports And Leisure

Fitness Club, Monthly Fee for 1 Adult	1,050.00 ฿
Tennis Court Rent (1 Hour on Weekend)	50.00 ฿
Cinema, International Release, 1 Seat	200.00 ฿

🛒 Childcare

Preschool (or Kindergarten), Full Day, Private, Monthly for 1 Child	15,833.33 ฿
International Primary School, Yearly for 1 Child	250,000.00 ฿

👕 Clothing And Shoes

1 Pair of Jeans (Levis 501 Or Similar)	1,800.00 ฿
1 Summer Dress in a Chain Store (Zara, H&M, ...)	800.00 ฿
1 Pair of Nike Running Shoes (Mid-Range)	2,600.00 ฿
1 Pair of Men Leather Business Shoes	2,066.67 ฿

🛏 Rent Per Month

Apartment (1 bedroom) in City Centre	7,333.33 ฿
Apartment (1 bedroom) Outside of Centre	4,125.00 ฿
Apartment (3 bedrooms) in City Centre	25,666.67 ฿
Apartment (3 bedrooms) Outside of Centre	17,000.00 ฿

🏢 Buy Apartment Price

Price per Square Meter to Buy Apartment in City Centre	?
Price per Square Meter to Buy Apartment Outside of Centre	?

Courtesy of www.numbeo.com

THE PEOPLE OF CHIANG RAI

One of the most popular aspects of Northern Thailand is the many Hill Tribes that live in the mountains in the surrounding areas. These people are migrants to Thailand having arrived a little over 100 years ago from China, Northern Burma and even Tibet, by various routes and for different reasons. There are many differences between the tribes, their dress, speech, rituals and attitudes. The largest of the hillside tribes is the Karen who came from Myanmar where they were persecuted for their beliefs. There are approximately 320,000 Karen in Thailand and comprise half of the country's total hill tribe population.

The Hmong are the second largest of the tribes in Thailand. The Hmong are located predominantly in the Thai Highlands, although some are found elsewhere within the country. Among the Hill Tribes, the Hmong are becoming well integrated into Thai society as well as being among the most successful of the tribes. The current population of Hmong in Thailand is estimated to be 150,000. As with the people of Chiang Mai, you will find the people of Chiang Rai to just as be friendly and helpful.

WHAT DOES CHIANG RAI OFFER FOR EXPATS LIVING THERE?

Being a smaller town the number of expats in Chiang Rai is much lower than in neighboring Chiang Mai. You won't see too many bars with lots of expats passing the time of day either. There is a Chiang Rai Expats Club, though it does not have its own clubhouse but organises events and gatherings in hotels and restaurants. There is also an Expat Ladies Group that meets on the first and third Tuesdays of every month. The first Tuesday meeting being an informal get-together at the Grand View Hotel, and the third Tuesday being a slightly more formal luncheon, held at a different venue each time.

***See Useful Website pages at the end of
this book for expat club links**

PLACES TO GO AND THINGS TO DO IN CHIANG RAI
Chiang Rai is the little sister of Chiang Mai and gets about a third of the tourists that Chiang Mai gets so the city has much the same to offer but on a smaller scale. The city's main claim to fame is the White Temple but the area has a lot more to offer than just one famous temple.

WAT RONG KHUN / THE WHITE TEMPLE
The White Temple attracts a large number of visitors, both Thai and foreign, making it Chiang Rai's most visited attraction. The Buddhist Temple is like no other temple in Thailand and is a paradox of both traditional Buddhist themes and modern influences, including murals of Mickey Mouse, Superman, Kung Fu Panda, Super Heroes and even Michael Jackson, all add to the intrigue and quirkiness of this famous temple and tourist attraction. The White Temple was created by master Chalermchai Kositpipat, the artist who designed,

constructed, and opened it to visitors in 1997. Before he took on the enormous project, the original Wat Rong Khun was in a bad state of repair and funds were not available for renovation. Chalermchai Kositpipat who was a local artist from Chiang Rai, decided to completely rebuild the temple and fund the project with his own money. To date, Chalermchai has spent well over a million Baht on the project. The artist intends for the area adjacent to the temple to be a centre of learning and meditation and for people to gain benefit from the Buddhist teachings. Kositpipat considers the temple to be his offering to Lord Buddha and believes the project will give him immortal life. It is a work in progress but even as it stands today it is a magnificent work of art.

THE GOLDEN TRIANGLE VIEWPOINT.

The Golden Triangle Viewpoint is about a 90-minute drive north of Chiang Rai. The views from the viewpoint stretch out across the three borders of Thailand, Laos, and Myanmar on the spot where three of Southeast Asia's biggest nations converge. To the east is Laos and to the north is Myanmar, which sits across the mighty Mekong River. The Golden Triangle is named as it lies at the heart of what was once the huge opium-growing area of the world that started in the 1950s. The Thai government succeeded in eradicating most of the commercial cultivation of opium in the early 1990s and the fields surrounding the farming areas below are now filled with coffee and rice crops. There are two museums close by that have information and memorabilia relating to the opium trade over the years and also a few shops and stalls selling souvenirs but not opium. There are some restaurants that sit along the banks of the Mekong River which is the twelfth-longest river in the world, with an estimated length of 5,000 kilometers that meanders through six countries China, Myanmar, Thailand, Lao, Cambodia and Viet Nam.

THE HILL TRIBE MUSEUM AND EDUCATION CENTRE.

The north of Thailand and the area surrounding Chiang Rai is home to numerous hill tribes, each with their own unique history, culture and traditions. The Hilltribe Museum is part of Chiang Rai's prominent ethnographic museum and cultural centre and chronicles the history of six hill tribes (Karen, Hmong, Yao, Lisu, Lahu, Lawa and Akha) who make their home in the surrounding Chiang Rai area. The complex is a great place to learn about Northern Thailand's hill tribes and the museum has a range of exhibits detailing their history and cultures where you can learn about how they came to make their home in Thailand, their customs, traditions and way of life. The museum aims to promote responsible tourism by educating visitors about Thailand's ethnic hill-tribe communities. The museum's souvenir shop offers regionally made handcrafts that reflect the hill tribes' heritage, including embroidered ornaments, woven baskets, and traditional costumes. By buying items you will be contributing to the preservation of their traditional way of life.

SINGHA PARK.

Singha Park is owned by Singha Brewery and was previously known as Boon Rawd Farm where the fertile soil was used to grow barley for brewing their beer production and the farm was off-limits to the general public. That all changed when the brewery decided to transform the area into a sustainable tourism project with Singha Park opening its gates to visitors in December 2012. Some areas around the park are still used as a working farm but now the fields are full of fruit orchards and tea plantations. The Park is a popular place for local Thais who like to go there to exercise and relax at the weekends but it has also been discovered by some of the tourists who come to Chiang Rai. You can spend a whole day or a few hours exploring this huge park and all it has to offer. Singha Park is worth a visit for all ages and is a great place for the whole family. The park features flower gardens, lakes, meadows, plantations, and vegetable crops. When you first arrive, you will see a giant golden lion statue at the entrance of the park, the same lion that is the symbol of Singha Beer, who chose it as a symbol of strength, courage, leadership, dignity, loyalty, perseverance, and endurance. As you enter the park you will find bicycles for hire which is the best way to get around and see everything that the vast park has to offer. Or you can hop on and off one of the electric trams to find your way around the park. There is a petting zoo with sheep, goats and other cute animals as well as giraffes and zebras. There are plenty of restaurants, food stalls and coffee shops within the park and even a bakery.

THE BAAN DAM MUSEUM.
The Baan Dam Museum or the Black House as it is also known is a private art museum and park containing a diverse series of buildings, displays, and sculptures that spans the ancient Lanna era and the modern. The museum and its eclectic displays are the life's work of the renowned local artist Thawan Duchanee.

CHIANG RAI CLOCK TOWER.
The Chiang Rai Clock Tower is one of the city's most unique attractions. The clock is the brainchild of renowned local Thai artist Chalermchai Kositpipat who designed the incredible White Temple, the clock has a unique design similar to some of the designs seen in the White Temple and sits in the centre of town in the middle of the road as a featured roundabout. The clock tower stands out during the day with its vibrant gold colour but there is a light projection show which occurs at seven, eight and nine o'clock each evening.

THE KAD LUANG CHIANG RAI MARKET.
The Kad Luang is a must-visit market if you would like to experience the true local food scene. The market has three floors

of freshly cooked food, but it also sells household goods and affordable clothing. The indoor-outdoor market caters to mostly locals, and it's a great way to experience how the locals live. As Kad Luang is a local market where local Thai locals do their shopping, expect to find similar goods that you see at other Markets but at much cheaper prices.

WHAT TO DO WHEN THE SUN GOES DOWN IN CHIANG RAI?

Chiang Rai has a vibrant nightlife but on a smaller scale than its neighbouring city Chiang Mai. The city has many expat bars and lady bars as you would expect in a moderately tourist city. There are also many night markets and food and dining opportunities from humble food stalls to 5-star dining experiences.

CHIANG RAI NIGHT MARKETS.
In the evening there are many night markets throughout the city. Most of them are in the more touristy areas like Old Town

THE CHIANG RAI NIGHT BAZAAR.
Although the night markets in Chiang Rai may not be as big and brash as those in Chiang Mai, they are still fun to explore and offer plenty of cheap food, clothing, handicrafts and souvenirs. One of the best markets is the Chiang Rai Night Bazaar which comes to life when the sun sets over the hills of Northern Thailand. The hundreds of stalls offer souvenirs, clothing, electronics, handmade jewellery, carved elephants and Buddha statues. Bargaining is expected, so brush up on your bargaining skills before you arrive. There are many food and drink stalls where you can choose what you fancy that night and then sit down and take in some of the shows when the singers and dancers take to the stage and put on a show into the night while you eat and drink. The market is situated on the south side of the downtown, within easy walking distance of most of the tourist hotels in the city and close to the main street in town, Phaholyothin Road.

SATURDAY WALKING STREET MARKET.

Saturday Walking Street which is the biggest night market in Chiang Rai is another night market that sets up shop in Chiang Rai when the sun is starting to go down. As the name implies it is only open on Saturdays. The market stretches the length of Thanon Thanalai Road in the heart of the city. Here you will find everything from high-end fashion knockoffs to local crafts and household goods. The market is also a good spot for local handmade shawls and batik fabrics and you will find many stalls with items made by the hill tribes, including some of their exquisite embroidery. As you would expect the market is occupied by open-air food stalls where you can sample many northern Thai delicacies, including fried insects and scorpions. There's a stage near the food court section where local artists perform live until late in the evening and you will also find street performers and musicians performing all over the night market.

HAPPY STREET MARKET.

Happy Street Market also known as Thanon Khon Muan Market is a market that pops up every Sunday evening with food, shopping, and live music. You'll find stalls selling the usual inexpensive souvenirs, clothes, shoes, wallets, toys, and games. The market is also a good choice if you want to buy produce from local farmers. While smaller than most of Chiang Rai's night markets, it's still worth a visit if you're in the area on a Sunday evening. There is no shortage of local food either with dozens of vendors serving up local Thai cuisine, including fried and BBQ meats, stir fry and rice and noodle dishes and the central stage often holds traditional Lanna cultural shows and performances by local musicians.

BARS AND NIGHTLIFE CHIANG RAI

Chiang Rai being the second most visited tourist area in Northwestern Thailand does have an exciting nightlife scene and also has a few lady bar areas scattered around the city. As in Chiang Mai, there are two kinds of bars in Chiang Rai there are your regular bars and then there are your Lady Bars. For your regular bars, there are many to choose from but the ones that stand out are worth checking out around the city. A lot of the Chiang Rai nightlife and nightclubs are found in the south of Chiang Rai near Phaholyothin Road though many of the foreigners and tourists go to the Jetyod Road area where there are many lady bars and happy ending massage shops and soapy massage shops.

SOME OF THE REGULAR BARS IN CHIANG RAI

REGGAE HOME AND BAR.
The Reggae Home and Bar is a great place to unwind after a hard day exploring the city and is one of the most popular bars in Chiang Rai with a huge number of locals and visitors frequenting the bar every night. Here you will find live music every night and also some jam sessions and open mic nights. As the name suggests reggae is the main theme but intersperses with jazz, rock, pop, and RnB. There are also pool tables and darts and they sometimes have competitions.

KAFFEE HUB.
The Kaffee Hub occupies a large historic building in the centre of Chiang Rai. It's a cafe that serves coffee by day, but the real fun starts in the evening when it comes alive as a bar and music venue. The bar has a good range of beers, plus a decent cocktail menu. Downstairs can sometimes be throbbing with live music while upstairs the balcony area tends to be quieter and more relaxing. The balcony is a great place to go to get a view of the Chiang Rai Clock Tower's evening light show.

TAMARIND BISTRO AND MUSIC HOUSE.
Tamarind Bistro and Music House is in two old wooden houses that are reputed to be over 50 years old. It is a café/restaurant during the day and transforms into a music venue at night. They

have a long list of cocktails and they also have a trendy food menu such as fried tofu with tamarind sauce and many shrimp and seafood dishes.

AUSSIE SPORTS BAR

It seems that wherever you go in Thailand you will find an Aussie bar and Chiang Rai doesn't disappoint either. The Aussie Sports Bar is the perfect combination of an entertainment place, where there are good beers on tap and large screen TVs screening different sports. This is a bar that is great for people of all ages. You can have a few drinks while watching football, playing billiards, or chatting with the locals or newly found friends. The walls and ceilings are decorated with cartoon characters and the ceilings are covered with many flags from the different countries of their many customers.

Many of the popular bars are located on Jetyod which is Chiang Rais "Pub Street" though far less intense than Khao San Road in Bangkok or the original "Pub Street" in Siem Reap in Cambodia. But the road is home to an increasing number of expat bars and daytime restaurants and comes to life at night, with a mixture of bars, pubs, restaurants, and live music venues. The atmosphere is laidback and you can walk the small soi and check out the many different bars to see what they have to offer. You can play pool at Chicken Bar or a game of ping-pong at the aptly named 69 Bar. For great beers from around the world, try the craft beers at the Bavarian Beer House or a glass of Guinness at O'Kane's Irish Pub. Other popular places to go are Rosebar and Dragon's Breath

.

LADY BARS IN CHIANG RAI

Jetyod Road south of the clock tower, is the area where you will find the most lady bars and where most farang and male tourists end up when looking to hook up with a Thai lady. There are around twenty lady bars and there's also a lady-boy bar, Bar Lamyai, that always seems to be busy with expats. The more frequented bars are Cat Bar, Get2Her Bar and Dragon Breath. As well as the bar girls on offer many of the bars offer free pool games and have large-screen TVs.

THE FOOD IN CHIANG RAI

For Thai people, food plays a big part in their socialising. Going to friends or family for a meal or out to a restaurant is something the Thais love to do. Chiang Rai is no exception. The food in Chiang Rai is one reason alone why you may want to call Chiang Rai home. Fresh vegetables and herbs play a big part in food preparation; this includes a lot of locally grown herbs, roots, bamboo shoots, wheat grass and lemon grass which make up some of the ingredients in a lot of their cuisine. Local Chiang Rai dishes include Kaeng Khanoon which is a curry made from the aromatic flesh of the Jack fruit. It is one of the most traditional curries from the north of the country. Khaeng Yuak is another traditional northern Thai dish. Yuak (banana trunk) are part of the recipe, only the tender part is used which comes from the centre part of the tree, chicken, glass noodles and sometimes dried fish are also part of the ingredients. If you are from the UK and you are in need of some food from your own country try Aye's Restaurant on Phaholyothin Road for tender Angus steaks, fish and chips or a full English breakfast. They also have an international menu as well as traditional Thai food.

CHIANG RAI'S HOSPITALS AND MEDICAL FACILITIES
Chiang Rai is a small city but still has moderately extensive medical facilities. There are three hospitals in Chiang Rai, one is the government-run Chiang Rai Prachanukhro Hospital, which is always very busy due to it being a public hospital. There are two private hospitals. Kasemrad Sriburin Hospital and the Overbrook Hospital. All three hospitals have emergency services. Kasemrad Sriburin is considered by most ex-pats that I have spoken with to be the best hospital. The hospital covers an extensive range of medical practices, including dental, and orthopaedic. obstetrics, gynaecology and heart centre. There are also the usual clinics and dental practices scattered around Chiang Rai City.

THE DOWNSIDES OF LIVING IN CHIANG RAI:
Being just a three-hour drive from Chiang Mai, Chiang Rai has

similar downsides to living there as its sister city.

THE LONG DISTANCE FROM EVERYWHERE ELSE IN THAILAND:

Chiang Rai is an eleven-hour drive to Bangkok and around a fourteen-hour drive to the nearest beach. Koh Samui is a twenty-one-hour drive plus a two-hour ferry crossing. Pattaya is a thirteen-hour drive and Phuket is a twenty-three-hour drive so Chiang Rai may seem off the beaten track and if you are coming to live here with the idea of regular travel around Thailand then you may find that Chiang Rai is quite remote.

THE POLLUTION IN THE BURN OFF-SEASON:

As in Chiang Rai and many other rural areas in Thailand every year between January to March and sometimes longer the area is infamously known as *The Burn-Off Season*. This is a time when the air quality in the area is one of the worst in the world over that period. This is the time of the year when local farmers burn off their fields from the previous year's crops to prepare their land for the following year's crops and to rid the fields of biowastes. In Thailand, it's illegal to burn the fields as it causes harm to the environment and people's health but the government turn a blind eye to it and allows it to happen each year to appease the struggling farmers. The pollution can spike to AQI 300+ and is particularly bad for young children the elderly, and people with respiratory diseases, such as asthma, emphysema and bronchitis and they should avoid being outdoors during this period.

LANGUAGE BARRIER:

Chiang Rai doesn't get as many foreign tourists as Chiang Mai so English is not widely spoken In the more touristy areas of the city, you will find more English is spoken but you may find that in the more remote parts of the city and the rural areas you will have difficulty with the language.

PATTAYA

CHAPTER EIGHT

PATTAYA

The resort city of Pattaya is about 150 kilometres southeast of Bangkok. Pattaya was just a small fishing village until the Vietnam War. It was then used by US troops on R&R from their US bases, and it has never looked back since. The beaches are now lined with resort hotels and high-rise condominiums. Pattaya Beach is the most popular area for tourists and where you will find most of Pattaya's infamous nightlife, Walking Street is the main place to party. Jomtien Beach is popular with ex-pats and retirees as it is far more relaxed than Pattaya Beach. Many of Pattaya's retired expats live in neighbourhoods such as the areas around Mapbrachan Lake as it's away from the hustle and bustle of downtown Pattaya; it's about eight kilometres inland from Pattaya City. Don't be put off by the reputation Pattaya has for the sex industry. It's only there if you want to visit, it's not compulsory. There are some magnificent areas away from the crazy area of Walking Street and its surrounds. Pattaya is perfect for retirees looking for an outdoor lifestyle with plenty of different activities to keep them busy, including golf, beaches, sailing, shopping, Thai cooking schools, dance lessons, water parks, and Thai language schools. There are over twenty golf courses around the Pattaya area. There is a train station with one train a day to and from Bangkok that takes about three and a half hours. Driving to Bangkok by car is approximately a two-and-a-half-hour journey. and there is also a regular bus service to the capital city. The border crossing to Cambodia at Krong Poi Pet is about a three-and-a-half-hour drive east and the beautiful island of Koh Chang in Trat is about

the same driving distance south

FACTS ABOUT PATTAYA

- Population: 120,000
- The climate of Pattaya can be divided into 3 main seasons: cool, hot and rainy and has a wet and dry climate throughout the year and is prone to

heavy rainfall. The weather becomes extremely hot and humid from March to May, and the temperature ranges around 33 degrees Celsius. The monsoon begins around July and extends up until October.

- Pattaya lies approximately 150 kilometres Southeast of Bangkok
- Pattaya is located in the province of Chonburi
- Pattaya was previously only known as a fishing village until the 1960s. when American servicemen fighting in the Vietnam War used the sleepy fishing town for R&R.
- Pattaya is a golfer's paradise with 23 golf courses scattered around the area
- Pattaya was previously called Tappaya but this was later changed to Phatthaya. It was later simplified to Pattaya when the city started to get popular with tourists.

THE WEATHER IN PATTAYA

The rainy season is between June and October Temperatures fluctuate in the low 30s during the day; and between 25c-27c at night.

The hot season runs between March and May with temperatures averaging highs of 33 degrees Celsius and lows of between 25c and 28c. The Cool Season (main tourist season) November through to February sees the perfect weather very little rain and hot but not too hot. Temperatures average highs of 31c and lows of around 21c-22c.

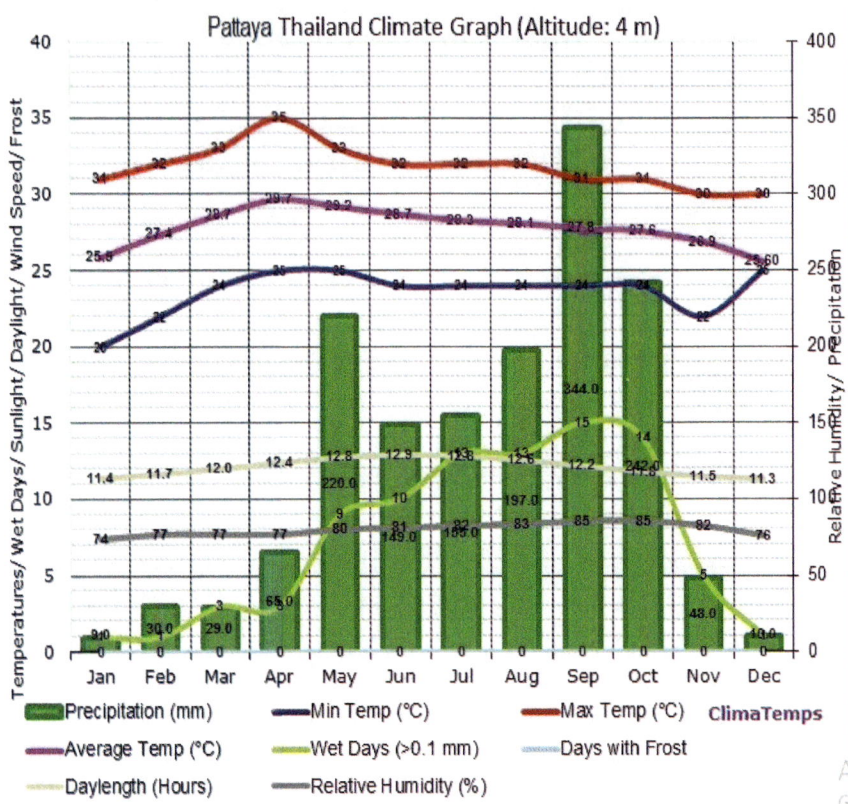

Courtesy of www.travelfish.com

PATTAYA'S COST OF LIVING

Food, transport, entertainment, utilities and healthcare are all very reasonable in Pattaya, Rents are a little less than comparative rentals in Bangkok. Pattaya is a booming tourist destination, as well as it is a favourite weekend getaway for Bangkok residents. Since COVID has been seen as a lesser concern to the Thai government and they have re-opened the country to foreign tourists once again prices are on the rise in the tourist areas. This is easily avoidable if you stay out of the main tourist area and shop where the locals shop.

Consumer Prices in Pattaya are 12.3% lower than in Bangkok (without rent)

Consumer Prices Including Rent in Pattaya are 18.5% lower than in Bangkok

Rent Prices in Pattaya are 34.7% lower than in Bangkok

Restaurant Prices in Pattaya are 3.4% higher than in Bangkok

Groceries Prices in Pattaya are 2.5% lower than in Bangkok

Local Purchasing Power in Pattaya is 9.7% lower than in Bangkok

✗ Restaurants

Meal, Inexpensive Restaurant	120.00 ฿
Meal for 2 People, Mid-range Restaurant, Three-course	1,000.00 ฿
McMeal at McDonalds (or Equivalent Combo Meal)	270.08 ฿
Domestic Beer (0.5 liter draught)	72.50 ฿
Imported Beer (0.33 liter bottle)	85.00 ฿
Cappuccino (regular)	66.45 ฿
Coke/Pepsi (0.33 liter bottle)	24.16 ฿
Water (0.33 liter bottle)	12.99 ฿

🛒 Markets

Milk (regular), (1 liter)	60.15 ฿
Loaf of Fresh White Bread (500g)	48.21 ฿
Rice (white), (1kg)	34.35 ฿
Eggs (regular) (12)	78.15 ฿
Local Cheese (1kg)	585.44 ฿
Chicken Fillets (1kg)	109.18 ฿
Beef Round (1kg) (or Equivalent Back Leg Red Meat)	535.89 ฿
Apples (1kg)	93.11 ฿
Banana (1kg)	47.40 ฿
Oranges (1kg)	76.12 ฿
Tomato (1kg)	46.88 ฿
Potato (1kg)	53.33 ฿
Onion (1kg)	33.75 ฿
Lettuce (1 head)	50.25 ฿
Water (1.5 liter bottle)	20.40 ฿
Bottle of Wine (Mid-Range)	600.00 ฿
Domestic Beer (0.5 liter bottle)	59.16 ฿
Imported Beer (0.33 liter bottle)	63.67 ฿
Cigarettes 20 Pack (Marlboro)	145.00 ฿

🚗 Transportation

One-way Ticket (Local Transport)	10.00 ฿
Monthly Pass (Regular Price)	600.00 ฿
Taxi Start (Normal Tariff)	40.00 ฿
Taxi 1km (Normal Tariff)	30.00 ฿
Taxi 1hour Waiting (Normal Tariff)	100.00 ฿
Gasoline (1 liter)	43.33 ฿
Volkswagen Golf 1.4 90 KW Trendline (Or Equivalent New Car)	850,000.00 ฿
Toyota Corolla Sedan 1.6l 97kW Comfort (Or Equivalent New Car)	859,666.67 ฿

🖫 Utilities (Monthly)

Basic (Electricity, Heating, Cooling, Water, Garbage) for 85m2 Apartment	2,585.13 ฿
Mobile Phone Monthly Plan with Calls and 10GB+ Data	517.09 ฿
Internet (60 Mbps or More, Unlimited Data, Cable/ADSL)	618.18 ฿

🚴 Sports And Leisure

Fitness Club, Monthly Fee for 1 Adult	1,439.90 ฿
Tennis Court Rent (1 Hour on Weekend)	377.00 ฿
Cinema, International Release, 1 Seat	200.00 ฿

🛒 Childcare

Preschool (or Kindergarten), Full Day, Private, Monthly for 1 Child	10,750.00 ฿
International Primary School, Yearly for 1 Child	300,000.00 ฿

👕 Clothing And Shoes

1 Pair of Jeans (Levis 501 Or Similar)	934.00 ฿
1 Summer Dress in a Chain Store (Zara, H&M, ...)	716.67 ฿
1 Pair of Nike Running Shoes (Mid-Range)	3,302.04 ฿
1 Pair of Men Leather Business Shoes	1,791.67 ฿

🛏 Rent Per Month

Apartment (1 bedroom) in City Centre	17,178.88 ฿
Apartment (1 bedroom) Outside of Centre	10,278.12 ฿
Apartment (3 bedrooms) in City Centre	32,089.75 ฿
Apartment (3 bedrooms) Outside of Centre	21,332.11 ฿

🏢 Buy Apartment Price

Price per Square Meter to Buy Apartment in City Centre	59,600.00 ฿
Price per Square Meter to Buy Apartment Outside of Centre	38,000.00 ฿

Courtesy of wwwnumbeo.com

WHAT DOES PATTAYA OFFER FOR EXPATS LIVING THERE?

Pattaya has a huge ex-pat community and a few expat clubs including, Pattaya Expats, Pattaya International Ladies Club, Pattaya Sports Club and Pattaya City Expats Club. It's reputed that there is more farang per square mile here than in any other city in Thailand. There is also a bowling green that attracts a lot of expats. As well as the expats there is also always a constant flow of western tourists coming through town, so you don't have to go far to hear voices from your home country. There is also the usual assortment of Brit, Irish, Aussie, Kiwi and USA bars and restaurants that always gather expats especially when there is a sporting event being screened.

***See Useful Website pages at the end of
this book for expat club links**

PLACES TO GO AND THINGS TO DO IN PATTAYA

POPULAR BEACHES OF PATTAYA

- Jomtien Beach
- Pattaya Beach
- Bang Saray Beach
- Wong Amat Beach
- Koh Larn Beach
- Tawaen Beach

JOMTIEN BEACH

Jomtien Beach is fringed by palm trees and is an ideal place to chill out with family and friends. If you get tired of lying on the beach the beachfront is lined with bustling shops, cafes, and restaurants offering sumptuous Thailand Western foods Jomtien is considered to be one of the best beaches in Pattaya.

PATTAYA BEACH

Pattaya Beach is about 2.7 km long and 25 metres wide running from Pattaya Nuea south to Walking Street. It lies parallel to the city. This place is perfect for long early morning or late afternoon walks along the coastline

.

BANG SARAY BEACH

Bang Saray is a stretch of sandy beach wedged between the narrow road lined with restaurants, hotels and food vendors and the warm waters of the Gulf of Thailand. The beach is popular with scuba divers and is a quieter and more inviting alternative to the urban beaches of Pattaya to the north. Though popular with tourists and locals the beach area still retains some of its former fishing village charm and seems a million miles away from the hustle and bustle of Pattaya.

WONG AMAT BEACH

Wong Amat Beach is located next to northern Pattaya Beach and is one of the cleanest and best beaches in Pattaya. The road behind the beach is lined with many luxurious sea-facing hotels and restaurants and is popular with families and people who want to avoid the more central busy Pattaya Beaches.

KOH LARN BEACH

With its transparent water and white sand Koh Larn Beach is one of the nicest beaches in Pattaya. The beach is accessed by a 15-minute ferry ride.

TAWAEN BEACH

Tawaen Beach is one of the most beautiful beaches in Pattaya. The blue seas with the lush green backdrop of the mountains behind make it a very relaxing place to escape the busier areas of Pattaya. As usual in beach areas when hunger strikes, you can head across the road to one of the many restaurants and food stalls serving Thai and international cuisine.

Pattaya for good reason, is renowned the world over for being the sex capital of Thailand and probably South East Asia so many of the people who come to holiday or live here do so for the seedy nightlife. But Pattaya has so much more to offer than just bars, girls and ladyboys.

PATTAYA VIEWPOINT
Pattaya Viewpoint also known as Khao Pattaya View Point on Pratumnak Hill, is the best viewpoint in the region and is a fantastic place to visit day or night to get a bird's eye view of the sweeping, crescent-shaped bay.

NONG NOOCH TROPICAL GARDEN
Nong Nooch Tropical Garden's sprawling grounds feature over 200 hectares of landscaped gardens bursting with tropical colours. The grounds have some of the most remarkable flowers, displays and landscaped gardens in Thailand. And repeatedly win international awards for their designs, which include 17th-century French-style gardens, a recreation of Stonehenge, creative topiary displays and gardens created exclusively with cacti, bonsais and tropical palms. It is also the home of over 670 native and hybrid species of orchids. You can see regular displays of classic Thai dancing, kickboxing and tribal drumming during your visit to the gardens.

THE SANCTUARY OF TRUTH
The Sanctuary of Truth is a one-of-a-kind teak structure in Pattaya and a truly awe-inspiring monument to philosophical

truth. It tells of the importance religion, philosophy and art have played in human development and the folly of neglecting morality and spiritual contentment in the pursuit of materialism. The complex is a beautiful and humbling demonstration of human endeavour and skill, particularly when you realise that none of the wood being used has been treated or chemically protected. This means that, as one section is completed, another has often succumbed to the conditions and must be replaced so it is an ongoing commitment.

PATTAYA FLOATING MARKET

Pattaya Floating Market, also known as The, Four Regions Floating Market, is a 10-hectare development that represents the four major areas of Thailand: the north, northeast, central, and south. This representation comes in the form of shops and stalls selling souvenirs, fruits, food, art, handicrafts, postcards and clothing as well as regular cultural shows and demonstrations. Some of the 114 vendors do indeed float, selling their wares from traditional boats and canoes. The rest are built into a sturdy stilted village, with covered walkways and stout bridges connecting them.

BIG BUDDHA TEMPLE

The Big Buddha Temple of Pattaya certainly lives up to its name, being the biggest Buddha statue in the region at 18 metres in height. As big as it is it is still dwarfed by Big Buddha in Phuket that sits overlooking the Gulf of Thailand at 45 meters in height. Big Buddha Pattaya is positioned 100 metres above sea level, between Pattaya and Jomtien Beaches. The full name of this stunning temple is Wat Phra Khao Yai, and the temple complex surrounds the highly detailed golden seated Buddha.

CORAL ISLAND

Coral Island is situated eight kilometres west of Pattaya Beach. And offers blue seas and a long stretch of a pristine golden beach and is a contrast to the main areas of Pattaya as it is void of high-rise buildings and away from the sometimes-claustrophobic atmosphere of Pattaya. Also known as Koh Laan or Larn Island, it's the main island of other similarly idyllic little islands known as the Near Islands because they are near Pattaya. Coral Island is the only island in the group of islands with any significant development such as roads, restaurants and shops. Coral Island has long been the retreat for those who have become jaded with Pattaya's overdeveloped and overcrowded beaches.

NAM TOK CHAN TA THEN WATERFALL

Located a scenic 90-minute drive from Pattaya, the Nam Tok Chan Ta Then Waterfall is the largest in the province. It's a great place to get out of the city and get back to nature.

The greenery is unending and the waterfall stretches for over 1 kilometre. So there's lots to explore and many different locations to sit! Picnicking is customary here, and you can even hire a picnic mat!

BUDDHA MOUNTAIN

Khao Chi Chan or Buddha Mountain in Jomtien is the largest engraving of Buddha in the world. The gold-embossed image is 130 metres in height and 70 metres across at its widest point. The limestone hill was once used to supply the local construction industry with limestone but in 1996, to commemorate His Majesty the King of Thailand's golden jubilee, the image was carved into the limestone cliff and then marked out in gold. The grounds in front of Buddha Mountain include a temple, with saffron-robed monks a common sight.

WHAT TO DO WHEN THE SUN GOES DOWN IN PATTAYA?

Pattaya is a carefree party town where people travel from all over the world to look for a great night out and perhaps more. Almost every area in the city has some form of nightlife, including live rock bands, international DJs, cabaret shows, pool parties and rooftop bars. You will find that some of Pattaya's infamous nightlife spots are family-friendly but most are not. There is a lot of variety to be found in and around the city, with radically different kinds of venues found throughout Pattaya.

WALKING STREET
Stretching from Pattaya Beach Road to Bali Hai Plaza, Walking Street is the epicentre of Pattaya's notorious red-light district, with pubs, nightclubs, go-go bars and massage parlours galore, and is unlike anywhere else in Thailand. While Walking Street in most other towns and cities around Thailand usually means a regular street market, that's not the case here. Indeed, there's almost nothing in the country that matches the 500 metres of the unabashed sex industry that is found at the end of Pattaya's Beach Road. Taking its name from the fact that it is closed to vehicle traffic after 6.00 pm every evening, almost every building on both sides of the road, as well as many in the side streets adjoining Walking Street, is a nightclub, bar or restaurant, to the extent that the road is almost completely deserted during daylight hours as virtually everything is closed until the evening when the street comes alive with neon lights, thumping music from different genres, food vendors, street performances and partygoers from around the world. There's something for everyone with lady bars, gay bars and ladyboy bars all around the area.

BEACH ROAD SOI SEVEN
On Soi Seven off Beach Road, you will find the pink-neon-lit beer bars are renowned for being a little on the seedy side, but the drinks here are far cheaper than they are around Walking Street. Because of this, the street is particularly popular with expat retirees and budget travellers, and a good place to have a few cheap drinks before you head for the more expensive clubs and

bars.

TIFFANY'S CABARET

Tiffany Pattaya was the first Transvestite Cabaret Show in Thailand and South East Asia and has been in operation for over 40 years. It is also Asia's biggest and most extravagant Cabaret, with a cast of many glamorous dancers, hilarious comedians and other performers, the show guarantees a fun, lively and varied night out.

HORIZON ROOFTOP RESTAURANT AND BAR

The Hilton Hotel dominates the city's skyline and is the tallest building on Pattaya Beach Road. On the 34th floor, you will find the Horizon Bar. It's a great place to enjoy a drink while taking in the stunning views while watching the sun go down.

THE SIAM@SIAM DESIGN HOTEL

The Siam@Siam Design Hotel has an assortment of bars and lounges of different styles. Watch the sunset by the infinity pool on the 25th floor which is home to some of the city's best pool parties. One floor below is The Roof Sky Bar & Restaurant which has a beachy feel to it. Car Bar on the ground floor is another great bar within the complex to unwind after a hard day at the beach.

THE HARD ROCK CAFE

The Hard Rock Cafes are recognised the world over for their eclectic style and great music. With the iconic giant guitar and their *No Drugs or Nuclear Weapons Allowed Inside* neon sign over the door to the collection of music and movie memorabilia, the place is a great way to spend some time. The music starts at 6.00 pm on the Sun & Moon deck, which looks out over Beach Road. The house band starts up at 9.30 pm and plays into the early hours. The excellent rock groups are frequently rotated, with special guest bands also making regular appearances. The attached Hard Rock Hotel also hosts some of the best foam parties in the region, the Miss Hard Rock beauty contest and the venue also hosts the annual guitar festival.

THAI KICKBOXING

If you are into the sport, Pattaya has many kickboxing venues scattered around the city areas such as Max Muay Thai and Pattaya Boxing World on Sukhumvit Road, see rising stars in the amateur leagues at the Thepprasit Kickboxing Stadium or take in a bout over a beer or two on Walking Street, in one of a few boxing rings scattered along the famous road surrounded by beer bars.

THE FOOD IN PATTAYA

Pattaya doesn't have its own local cuisine but does offer fantastic food to suit all tastes and budgets. Pattaya started as a small fishing village and still has hundreds of fishing boats that fish overnight to feed the local population and tourists who crave fresh seafood. Moom Aroi is a highly-rated seafood restaurant that sits right on the beach in Naklua. Frequented by local Thais and in-the-know expats, the fresh local seafood on offer is straight from the morning's catch. Another great seafood restaurant that's also on the beach is Lungsawai Seafood in Jomtien. Being a city that attracts tourists from all around the world, you will find many country's restaurants represented here. Not just the usual Chinese, Italian, French and USA burger joints, but restaurants serving Russian, Turkish, Spanish Tapas, and African and South American cuisine. Street food of course is an important feature in Pattaya's food culture. You are never more than a couple of minutes away from street food in Pattaya.

Classic Thai Street food dishes are often dishes that can be cooked quickly. You will find a fantastic selection of local dishes such as fried rice, Pad Thai, stir-fried noodles, noodle soup, barbecued meats, chicken skewers and sausages. Be warned some of these dishes can be very spicy as many street food vendors cater mainly for Thai people. If you think a dish might be too spicy for you just say mi phed (not spicy). Another great place for Thai food is the Thepprasit Weekend Night Markets. The aromas of Thai curries and smoky BBQs are irresistible.

PATTAYA'S HOSPITALS AND MEDICAL FACILITIES

There are five main hospitals in Pattaya, three of them are private and two are government hospitals, all with 24-hour emergency centres. Most of them have a dental department within the hospital. As usual in Thailand, many doctors are Western-trained and speak fluent English. Access to Bangkok's many hospitals is only a two-and-a-half-hour drive away. Pattaya has many dental practices and pharmacies where the majority of the staff will speak English.

Pattaya hospitals are:

The Bangkok Hospital

Pattaya International Hospital

Pattaya City Hospital

Pattaya Memorial Hospital

Banglamung Hospital

THE DOWNSIDES OF LIVING IN PATTAYA:

PATTAYA IS THE SEX CAPITAL OF THAILAND

Pattaya is classed as the sex capital of Thailand so if you're a of the male species and single then living in Pattaya you run the risk of being viewed as a sex tourist.

PATTAYA GETS VERY BUSY AT WEEKENDS AND BUDDHIST HOLIDAYS

As in Hua Hin, one of the good things about living in Pattaya is its proximity to Bangkok should you want a city break or if you are returning to your own country for a holiday and you are flying out of Bangkok. The problem is, that that can also have a downside, as on weekends, public holidays and Buddhist holidays hordes of Bangkokians head to Pattaya to escape the overbearing heat and the air pollution that tends to engulf the city.

CRIME AND SAFETY

Most times that I read or hear about someone getting mugged, beaten up, or being injured or killed in a motorbike accident it has quite often occurred in Pattaya. With Pattaya being the Sex Capital of not just Thailand, but probably the whole of Southeast Asia the city does tend to attract the wrong kinds of people so the crime rate is much higher there than the other seven places that I recommend as good places to live or retire to. Because of

Pattaya's reputation, many Lady Boys are attracted to ply their trade in Pattaya in the bar areas and along the shores of Pattaya Beach and some of them accost foreign tourists and steal wallets or jewellery...so be warned

CHAPTER NINE

HELPFUL TIPS AND IDEAS

- A good idea is to scan and put all of your important documents onto a USB flash drive so you have the information when you are anywhere overseas. I have my passport, driver's license, birth certificate, medication information and lots of other essential information in a safe place on a USB flash drive that I travel with at all times. That way if ever I lose my passport or driving license I have a copy, and will have that document reissued much more quickly.
- Download a Thai Baht currency converter cheat sheet from an online foreign exchange website such as Oanda. Shrink it to fit in your wallet or purse. This will give you a rough guide to what your home currency is worth against the Baht at a glance. But remember to update it regularly as exchange rates fluctuate often. Alternatively, download a currency converter app to your phone.
- "Leave the back door open". As much as Thailand is a fantastic country to retire to, it does not suit everyone. What you may have seen here on holiday is not always the reality of living here permanently. There are many reasons why some ex-pats can't settle and return home. Missing family and friends are the main reasons some retirees decide to pack up and return home. Other reasons are the climate, as lovely as it is waking up to sunshine most mornings, some people miss the seasons they get in

their own countries or just can't stand the constant heat or the wet season. Another reason is just plain old homesickness. It probably won't happen to you, but better to be safe than sorry. Rent for at least one year before you decide if you want to buy. If you have sold your property in your home country, perhaps put the funds in a term deposit until you are sure that you are settled in Thailand or until you are ready to buy a property here.

• Crime against foreigners in Thailand is rare but it does happen. If you follow the same rules you applied back home then you should be safe. Don't carry too much cash or flash your money around. Avoid going into remote and dark areas. Lock and secure your doors and windows when leaving your property. Try not to use the ATM at night, especially in unlit areas and when you're alone. Use your common sense as you did in your home country, Thailand is safe when compared to most emerging countries and in the six years I have lived here I have never had a serious problem.

• Phone charges are relatively cheap these days but it's even better when it's free. Get a free app on your phone and computer. You will be able to talk, send messages and even have a video link so that you can see your family and friends and they can see you while talking 24 hours a day. Many companies have this app, the main ones being Skype, Viber and Line. Line is the popular choice for most Thais. You can download the apps free with Google Apps or Play Store. I make most of my overseas calls, texts and local calls on Viber and Line for free.

• If you find a place to live that has all of the facilities you need close by, you might decide not to buy a vehicle, and rent when you need one. You can rent a motorbike by day, week or month for a very good price. This will save you money on the upkeep of a vehicle over the year such as maintenance, insurance and registration fees. If you prefer a car there are many car hire companies throughout Thailand. You may have to shop around if you only want a car for a day as the larger companies don't like daily rentals, though many of the smaller companies don't seem to mind.

Driving in Thailand
***A word of warning about driving a motorbike in Thailand

Many tourists come to Thailand and rent motorbikes. Most of them have a car driving license, not a motorbike driving license and they either know it's illegal to drive a motorbike on a car license but choose to bend the rules anyway or they assume that it's okay to drive here on a car license...it's not. As in your own country, you need a motorbike license to drive a motorbike here not a car driving license. The company that rents you the motorbike won't tell you this and they are happy to rent it to you even if you don't have the proper driving license as in their eyes it's up to you to know the laws of driving in Thailand and if they were to go by the rules, they wouldn't be able to rent many motorbikes because most tourists don't have a motorbike license. If the police pull you up, they will probably *"fine you"* 500 Baht for driving a motorbike with the wrong license and then let you drive away without any more problems. The problem may come later though if you are involved in a traffic accident and need hospital treatment, as your travel or medical insurance will deny your claim because you were driving unlicensed. I see it in the newspapers or on the internet every day when someone in Thailand or elsewhere in Southeast Asia has had a bad accident and has been hospitalised and their families are trying to raise money on GoFundMe to pay for their hospital treatment or bring their loved one home as their insurance company has disallowed the claim because the person was driving a motorbike on a car driving license. You should also know that if you drive here, you should have an International Driving License or a Thai driving license not just a license from your own country, though the police, if they are in a good mood that day, sometimes turn a blind eye to it if you're pulled up. It's also against the law here to drive without a motorbike without a crash helmet, though I would say at least 50% of motorbike drivers don't wear a helmet but they do wear face masks when riding motorbikes...go figure. I see many expats and foreign tourists also not wearing helmets because they see that most Thais aren't wearing one and that the police don't seem to care but I see in the newspapers over here on a regular basis where a foreign motorbike driver has been killed in a motorbike accident and had not been wearing a helmet.

***So have the right driving license and wear a helmet if you intend on driving a motorbike here. It could save you a lot of money and maybe your life.**

I have driven in Thailand for many years while holidaying in the country, and now living here for nearly seven years. Over that time, I have driven the length and breadth of the country on motorbikes and in cars and I have had two fairly serious road accidents, so driving here comes with risks that you may not find in your own country. Over the years I have learned a lot about the Thai version of the rules of the road. At first, it doesn't appear that there are any road rules, but when you see the chaos around you, you will probably think that you couldn't possibly drive here. But believe it or not, there is a method in the madness and you soon learn to adapt and what to expect on the roads of the unexpected but occasionally things do go wrong.

Here are a few driving tips to help you when you first arrive.

- Always wear a crash helmet; I would say that about 50% of motorcycle riders here don't wear a helmet. I have seen on many occasions ex-pats with two adults and three children on one motorbike doing about 80 kilometres an hour without any of them wearing a helmet. It's disturbing that many of the tourists and ex-pats here think that accidents only happen to other people and that they and their families are immune to accidents, and decide not to wear a helmet, even though they would not consider riding without one in their home country.

· When buying a helmet, it's a good idea to buy a crash helmet with headphones already fitted. That way you can download an app like Google Maps onto your phone. You can then get driving directions through headphones in most areas of Thailand. Obviously, have your headset volume at a level that you can still hear traffic around you. Many accidents are caused by drivers not knowing where they are going and making a quick rash decision when they realise that they have passed their turnoff. The Google Map App gives you turn-by-turn directions about five hundred meters before you need to make a decision. It can also direct you to petrol stations, banks, restaurants, in fact, any address or place you want to go in Thailand. Also, many road signs and direction signs are written only in Thai, which makes it difficult if you don't know where you're going and are looking for road signs for directions.

· Thailand is inundated with tourists and a lot of accidents are caused by motorcyclists who have no idea where they are going, they change direction without indicating when they see something of interest. Some tourists from Europe, the USA, and Canada are used to driving on the right-hand side of the road (they drive on the left here) and they sometimes find it hard to adjust when they first start riding on the left.

· Always double-check your rearview mirrors and indicate before changing lanes and changing lanes slowly. Motorbikes here tend to speed past either side of you.

- Beeping your horn here is not always considered bad form; a courteous beep is used to make another driver aware of your presence.
- Always pay attention to the vehicle in front of you and not so much to the people behind you unless you are changing lanes or turning. Drivers often change lanes without as much as a glance in their rearview mirrors.
- Look out for cars and motorbikes coming towards you on the wrong side of the road. Thai motorbike riders especially tend to find a break in the traffic, and then cross to the other side of the road. They then continue up the wrong side of the road into oncoming traffic until they reach their destination or turn off.
- Roundabouts are just a free-for-all unless the police are in the area and happen to be controlling traffic. If there is lots of traffic using the roundabout I always wait until a car is going in the same direction that I'm going and I drive parallel with the car until the car exits the roundabout, that way I am protected from oncoming traffic by the car.
- As a pedestrian don't even think about stepping onto the zebra crossing unless there is no traffic coming in either direction. Thai drivers do not believe that zebra crossings are for pedestrians, just zebras and you don't see many of them here. The same with traffic lights, even if you have the right of way, check in all directions before heading through the junction. It is not uncommon for drivers to go through an intersection or road junction without even looking for oncoming traffic or pedestrians.
- Always keep a lookout for vehicles suddenly pulling out even if they don't have the right of way.
- When driving a motorbike keep your bike at least

a car door width away from you. Thai drivers are notorious for opening their car doors without looking at what is coming behind them and they just throw open the door, sometimes with horrific consequences.

- In 2019 which was the year before covid arrived in Thailand, there were over 20,000 people who died from road accidents and 69 of them were foreign tourists.

BEACH SAFETY

At beaches always swim between the flags if flags are present but don't get complacent as unlike countries like Australia and the USA where beaches with flags mean that the beach is patrolled by lifeguards here in Thailand they are not always patrolled, in fact, most times they are not. Thailand's beaches are known for their rips, where even strong swimmers can get pulled out to sea. Learn how to get out of a rip if you are caught in one. This entails not panicking, by conserving your energy and swimming parallel to the shore, along the beach and then following the breaking waves back to shore at an angle, (swim to your left or right), don't try to swim in a straight line back to the beach if you are caught in a rip.

Be very wary of Parasailing in Thailand. The Thai laws governing the boating and maritime industry are very relaxed. When I first arrived in Thailand and was living in Phuket, two foreign tourists died in separate Parasailing accidents on the island. Since then, have seen news articles about other parasailing accidents within the country. It's probably very safe to Para-sail in most Western countries but personally, I would not take the risk here in Thailand.

Nine foreign tourists drowned on Thailand's beaches last year. The statistics on road deaths and swimming deaths are not meant to alarm you. If you follow the simple rules, you should be OK. It's the people who believe that the rules don't apply to them that get into difficulty and sometimes pay the ultimate price.

A FEW TIPS ON THE CULTURE OF THAILAND

- The king of Thailand is revered by the Thai people. Never make jokes or say anything uncomplimentary about the King or any of the Royal family. Unlike countries like the UK where you are allowed to show your dislike for the royal family if you so wish without any comeback, in Thailand, it's considered treason and you can end up in jail for a long time and a hefty fine under the *Lese Majeste Law* if you say the wrong thing.
- Try not to talk about Thai politics; it's a very touchy subject here as the country has had more than 10 military coup d'états since 1945 and it is best avoided.
- Avoid criticizing or getting angry with Thai people. Thai people hide their feelings to "save face" and making a Thai person lose face can end up very badly for you as an ex-pat and a guest in their country. Thais are a very proud people and if you treat them with dignity, you will find that they will respond to you in a much better manner. Insult them and you will not be welcome in their company again.
- Smile a lot, you're in the land of smiles and Thai people want to see you happy. We are in their country, and if they can smile even though many of them have very little to smile about compared to us farang, then so should we.
- Learn to speak at least some of the basics of the Thai language. The more you can communicate in Thai the more you will fit in and be accepted.
- Before visiting a Buddhist Temple make sure you know the etiquette required to enter the temple.

Dress appropriately, and remove your shoes when entering the main temple. Watch what the Thai people are doing, or if in doubt ask a Thai person what to do. Never disrespect a Buddha statue, and don't ever sit on one or put your arm around one for a photo opportunity. Turn off mobile phones, lower your voice, and don't use bad language or engage in improper conversations.

DEALING WITH THE HEAT, HUMIDITY AND THE WET SEASON

The chances are if you're retiring to Thailand you're coming from a cooler climate with more temperate seasons. To enjoy all of what Thailand has to offer it's important for you to be able to deal with the Thai weather and humidity. You will get acclimatised to the weather after your first few months here and get used to the heat and humidity.

A few hints on how to stay cool, dry and hydrated.

- In the wet season the humidity can be very high, it's the type of heat where you walk outside and instantly start sweating. Wear thin lightweight, loose-fitting clothes, made from cotton, not nylon.
- Even if it's not raining, I keep a lightweight rain jacket with me on my motorbike at all times in the wet season. It can be bright sunshine when you leave home and an hour later there's monsoon rain.
- It's usually cooler to cover your skin from the sun, in loose-fitting tops than it is to wear clothes that expose your body to the sun and risk sunburn.
- When you first arrive in Thailand or if your skin burns easily don't expose your skin to too much sun by wearing shorts, singlets and open-toed sandals or flip flops. Use a powerful sunblock on any exposed skin.
- Wear a sun hat and good Polaroid sunglasses.

- When out in the sun walk on the shady side of the street if possible and walk slowly.
- If going to the beach rent a chair with a sunshade so you have some protection when you need it.
- Stay hydrated and drink lots of water over the day and avoid alcohol and sugary fizzy drinks. If you're going out for the day and will not be close to any shops take plenty of bottled water with you. Freeze some of the bottles overnight so that they stay cooler over the day.
- Try to do physical work, exercise or any errands in the morning or late afternoon when it is much cooler.
- If you're at home feeling the heat, take frequent cool showers. If you have access to a swimming pool jump in and then sit in a shady spot.
- Try not to get too used to the air conditioning as not only is it expensive to run you can get too used to it and it then feels even hotter when you go outside, so utilise electric fans instead. Having said that, if you're out and about and struggling with the heat, pop into a shopping centre and take advantage of their free air conditioning.
- Try to stay out of the sun during the middle of the day when the sun is at its hottest and don't over-exert yourself.
- If you have air conditioning in your bedroom, switch it on half an hour before you go to bed and close the door to keep the cold air in. When you go to bed, switch on an electric fan and turn off the air-conditioning. Not only will it save you money it is more health efficient.

I am sure you will love living or retiring in Thailand; it's a magical place with so much to see and do. Then you have the rest of South East Asia to take in, right on your doorstep. Just take your time. Treat it like an extended holiday until you find the right place for you. You're retired now, this is your time to enjoy life to the fullest and being in Thailand you now have the time, money and resources to do just that.

HAVE A GREAT RETIREMENT YOU'VE EARNED IT!

**SOME THAI WORDS AND PHRASES TO
LEARN BEFORE YOU ARRIVE.**

If you are coming to Thailand and travelling through the not-so-touristy areas it may be good for you to be able to communicate a little so here are some Thai phrases and words to try to learn before you arrive.

THAI GREETINGS
Hello = Sawasdee Kah (for a female)
Hello = Sawasdee Krab (For Male)
How are you? = Sabaaidii mai?
I'm fine = Sabaaidii

I'm not well = Mai sabaii

I come from America = Pom/Chan maa jaak Ameerigaa

What country are you from? = Kun maa jaak bprateet arai?

Thank you = Khop kun

Sorry = Khot hort

No problem = Mai bpenrai

Goodbye = Bai

Can you speak English? = Kun pood paasaa anggrit dai mai

What is your name? = Kun chuu arai?

My name is __ = Pŏm / Chán chuu __.

THAI QUESTIONS

Where? = Tiinai?

What? = Arai?

When? = Muarai?

How? = Yangngai?

Why? = Tum mai?

ADDRESSING PEOPLE

I (female) = Chán

I (male) = Pŏm

You = Kun

He/She/They = Kao

Female/Male (junior) = Nong

Female/Male (senior) = Pee

DIRECTIONS AND TRANSPORT

Speak slowly = Puut chaa chaa noi

Do you use the meter? = Chai meter mai (Be sure taxi drivers use the meter in Bangkok!)

Nearby = Glai glai

Go straight = Dtrong bpai

Go left = Leo saai

Go right = Leo kwaa

Stop = Yut

Go to the airport = Bpai sanam bin

Station = Sataanii

Bus stop = Bpaai rot mee

Bus = Rot mee

Skytrain = Rodfai faa
Subway = Rodfai dtaaidin
Airplane = Kruang bin
Minibus = Rot dtuu
Car = Rot
Bicycle = Jakgrayaan
Motorcycle = Moodteesai
Boat = Rua

SHOPPING

How much? = Taorai
Very expensive = Paang mak
Can you reduce the price? = Lod noi dai mai
I want this one = Ao annii

THAI NUMBERS

1 = Nung
2 = Song
3 = Sam
4 = See
5 = Haa
6 = Hok
7 = Jet
8 = Bpeet
9 = Gaao
10 = Sip
20 = Yii sip
21 = Yii sip et
22 = Yee sip song
30 = Sam sip
40 = See sip
50 = Haa sip
60 = Hok sip
70 = Jet sip
80 = Bpeet sip
90 = Gaao sip
100 = Nung rooi
500 = Haa rooi

1,000 = Nung pan

EATING

Restaurant = Raan aahaan

Café = Raan gaafee

Excuse me = koortoot

Bathroom = Hongnaam

What is this? = Annii arai

Hungry = Hiu

May I have the menu = Aow meenuu noi

Vegetarian = Mawng sa vee rat

Vegan = Gin jay

Water = Naam

Beer = Beer (easy, right?)

Chicken = Gai

Rice = Kaao

Cold = Yen

Hot = Rone

No ice = Mai aow nam khang

No sugar = Mai aow nam tan

1 more please = Khor iik nung

I like spicy = Chan/Pom chawp pet

Not spicy = Mai pet

EMERGENCY

Hurts = Jep

Where is the police station? = Sataanii dtamruat yoo tee nai

Where is the hospital? = Rongpayaabaan yoo tee nai

Call an ambulance = Dahm rot pa-ya-bahn

I'm lost = Long tahng

Can you help = Choo-ay dai mai

A NIGHT OUT

Single = Bpen soht

Would you like a drink = Ja deum arai mai

I'm drunk = Mow

Cheers = Chon gâew

DAYS OF THE WEEK
Monday: Wan jan
Tuesday: Wan anghan
Wednesday: Wan phuut
Thursday: Wan paruuhat (
Friday: Wan suk
Saturday: Wan sow
Sunday: Wan ahtit

SOME GREAT QUOTES ON RETIREMENT

"What do you call someone who's happy on Mondays? Retired!" ~ Unknown
"The company gave me an aptitude test and I found out the work I was best suited for was retirement." ~ Unknown
"When a man retires, his wife gets twice as much husband for half as much money." ~ Chi Chi Rodriguez
"You have to put off being young until you can retire." ~ Unknown
"There are some who start their retirement long before they stop working." ~ Rober Half
"In your retirement years never drink coffee at lunch; it will keep you awake in the afternoon." ~ Unknown
"Retirement is not in my vocabulary. They aren't going to get rid of me that way." ~ Betty White
"I'm not just retiring from the company, I'm also retiring from my stress, my commute, my alarm clock, and my iron." ~ Hartman Jule
"Retirement: that's when you return from work one day and say 'hi honey, I'm home – forever'." ~ Gene Perret
"Some of the best memories are made in flip flops." ~ Kellie Elmore
"Often when you think you're at the end of something, you're at the beginning of something else." ~ Fred Rogers
"You are never too old to set another goal or to dream a new dream."

~ C. S. Lewis

"Planning to retire? Before you do, find your hidden passion – do the thing that you have always wanted to do." ~ Catherine Pulsifer

"It's time to say goodbye, but I think goodbyes are sad, and I'd much rather say hello. Hello to a new adventure." ~ Ernie Harwell

"Don't cry because it's over – smile because it happened." ~ Dr. Seuss

"Retirement is a blank sheet of paper. It is a chance to redesign your life into something new and different." ~ Patrick Foley

"Dare to live the life you have dreamed for yourself. Go forward and make your dreams come true." ~ Ralph Waldo Emerson

"Don't simply retire from something; have something to retire to." ~ Harry Emerson Fosdick

"What we call the beginning is often the end. And to make an end is to make a beginning. The end is where we start from." ~ T. S. Eliot

"Retirement is when you stop living at work and start working at living." ~ Unknown

SOME USEFUL WEBSITES

MY YOUTUBE CHANNEL ON LIVING IN THAILAND

https://tinyurl.com/4yysct8e

MY AUTHOR WEBSITE

https://tinyurl.com/366aw9jf

EXPAT ASSOCIATIONS THAILAND
www.escapethailand.com
www.internations.org
CHIANG MAI EX-PAT CLUBS
www.chiangmaiexpatsclub.com
www.chiangmaibuddy.com
PHUKET EXPAT CLUBS
www.meetup.com/Phuket-Dramatic-Arts-TheatreMeetup
www.meetup.com/Expats-in-Phuket-Meetup
www.phuketgoms.org grumpy old men
Hua Hin EXPAT CLUBS
www.huahinexpatnews.com (Advertises ex-pat events)
BANGKOK EXPAT CLUBS
www.britishclubbangkok.org
www.meetup.com/Bangkok-Expats
www.angloinfo.com/bangkok/directory/listing/bangkok-bangkokcosmopolitan-lions-club-international-8748

www.bangkokexpatlife.com/2015/09/best-places-tomeet-ex-pats-in-bangkok
KOH SAMUI EXPAT CLUB
www.ksh3.com (Hash House Harriers)
www.sistersonsamui@gmail.com
PATTAYA EXPAT CLUBS
www.pattayaretired.com
www.pattayaexpatsclub.info/wp
ww.pattayacityexpatsclub.com
www.meetup.com/cities/th/pattaya
www.pattayacityexpatsclub.com
LIMITED COMPANIES INFORMATION AND USUFRUCT
www.pricesanond.com/knowledge/corporate-m-and-a/steps-to-incorporate-a-private-limited-company-in- thailand.php
www.thailand-lawyer.com/usufruct.html
www.bangkokattorney.com/usufruct-in-thailand.html
HOSPITALS CHIANG MAI

www.lanna-hospital.com
www.rajavejchiangmai.com
www.bangkokhospital-chiangmai.com
www.chiangmairam.com
www.nkp-hospital.go.th (Government-Hospital)

HOSPITALS / BANGKOK

www.bumrungrad.com
www.bangkokhospital.com
www.samitivejhospitals.com
www.ram-hosp.co.th Ramkhamhaeng Hospital

HOSPITALS PHUKET

www.dibukhospital.com
www.phukethospital.com   (Bangkok   Hospital)
www.patonghospital.com
www.phuketinternationalhospital.com
www.vachiraphuket.go.th (Government Hospital)

HOSPITALS HUA HIN

www.sanpaulo.co.th
www.huahinhospital.go.th   (Government   Hospital)
www.bangkokhospital.com

HOSPITALS KRABI

www.krabihospital.go.th(GovernmentHospital)
www.krabinakharin.co.th

HOSPITALS CHIANG RAI

www.crhospital.org
www.overbrook-hospital.com
www.kasemrad.co.th

HOSPITALS KOH SAMUI

www.thaiinterhospital.com
www.sih.co.th Samui International Hospital
www.bangkokhospitalsamui.com
www.bangkokhospitalsamui.com/

HOSPITALS PATTAYA

https://www.pattayamemorial.com/
https://www.bangkokpattayahospital.com/en/

ENGLISH LANGUAGE NEWSPAPERS

www.nationmultimedia.com
www.bangkokpost.net
www.phuketgazette.net
www.chiangmai-mail.com
www.chiangraitimes.com
www.expathuahin.com
www.huahintoday.com
www.krabi-magazine.com/
www.krabi.uk/english-language-newspapers-andmagazines-in-krabi
www.thailandnews.co www.pattayamail.com
www.pattayatoday.net
www.pattayadailynews.com
www.patayainfo.com

VISA SERVICES

www.siam-legal.com
www.expressvisadirect.com
www.thaiimmigration.net
www.speedy-visa.com

THAILAND GOVERNMENT

www.thaiembassy.org (List of Embassy's Worldwide)
www.immigration.go.th
www.en.customs.go.th
www.dlt.go.th/en (Department of Transport)
www.driving-in-thailand.com/land-transport-officesin-thailand

BANKS

www.krungsri.com/bank/en/home.html
www.kasikornbank.com
www.bot.or.th/English/Pages/default.aspx(Bangkok Bank)
www.scb.co.th/en/home (Siam Commercial Bank)
www.citibank.co.th

MEDICAL INSURANCE

www.aetnainternational.com/ai/en/solutions/individuals
www.axa.co.th/en/international-exclusive
www.thaihealth.co.th/2012/product_wealthy_eng.php

www.bupa.co.th/en/individuals.aspx
www.thailand-health-insurance.com/insurers/allianz/
www.expatfinder.com/
www.expatfinder.com/landing-thailand-healthinsurance

CARS AND MOTORBIKES FOR SALE & RENT

www.motors.co.th/en/bikeslikecars.com
www.marketplacethailand.com/Motorbikes
www.thailand.carbay.com/en/motorcycles
www.bahtsold.com www.craigslist.co.th

PETS

www.8milesfromhome.com/post/23668603393/exporting-a-dog-from-uk-to-thailand

www.thailandstarterkit.com/moving/thailand-petimport
www.bangkok.craigslist.co.th/search/pet
www.th.locanto.asia/Dogs/803/ (Pets for sale)
www.soidog.org / (Pet shelter)
www.expat.com (Pet shelter)

WOMENS EXPAT AND SOCIAL CLUBS

www.chickynet.com/thailand/pages/phuket-expatwomen
www.bwgbangkok.org / British Women's Group Bangkok
www.iwcthailand.org / International Women's Club
www.awcthailand.org / Thailand American Women's Club (Newcomers Club)
www.anzwg-bangkok.org Australian-New-Zealand Women's Club
www.bwgbangkok.org / British Woman's Group

ABOUT THE AUTHOR

Gerald is originally from the UK. He has travelled the world working in 5-star hotels, restaurants, cruise ships, Antarctic supply ships, custom patrol vessels, rig tenders, and oil tankers. In the capacity of his work as a chef, he has also lived in Jamaica, Bermuda, Singapore, The Falkland Islands, Papua New Guinea, the Philippines and the USA. He has now retired in Thailand, where he lives in Hua Hin and travels extensively throughout SE Asia. His first book The Retire in Thailand Handbook, The first six months was published in January 2018. In 2021 Gerald started his YouTube channel about living and retiring in

Thailand.

BOOKS BY THIS AUTHOR

THE RETIREES TRAVEL GUIDE SERIES

The Retire in Thailand Handbook (The First Six Months)

My first six months in Thailand were frustrating. When I dreamed about retiring in Thailand, I thought that when I arrived, I would get my retirement visa, rent a condo, buy a vehicle, and then spend my time exploring my new country, going to the beach, going out for meals and meeting new friends. Unfortunately, reality took over and I spent most of my time dealing with Thai bureaucracy and trying to sort out the endless problems that arise when moving to a new country. Back in Australia I already had a visa, my own house, my own car, medical insurance, driver's license, bank accounts, credit rating, doctor and dentist. Moving to another country I was more or less starting my life over and I needed to establish myself within the Thai system. Government, banking, medical, everything that was just part of my everyday life at home, I had to re-create in Thailand. Hopefully, this book will give you the information you need to avoid most of the problems that I had, and allow you to retire to this wonderful country with confidence and assurance as well as save you time, money and your sanity. I wish I had been able to read this book before I left Australia.

The Retire in Thailand Handbook 2023…The Next Six Years

This book is a follow-up to the original book I wrote and published in 2017 on living or retiring in Thailand, The Retire in Thailand Handbook…The First Six Months. The book covers the six years I have lived here and guides the reader through the procedures and protocols of establishing yourself in a new country to live or retire. My target audiences are retirees or ex-pats who may want to come and live in Thailand where their money will stretch much further than in their home countries, The book is crammed full of advice on all aspects of establishing yourself in a new country, including:

- What to bring, and what not to bring to Thailand with you.
- How to apply for a Retirement Visa from your own country.
- How to apply for a Retirement Visa from within Thailand.
- How to open a Thai bank account

- How to transfer your pension to your new Thailand bank to avoid bank fees.
- How to buy a vehicle.
- How to apply for a Thai driving licence.
- How to rent a condo or a house.
- How to buy a property in Thailand.
- How to obtain suitable medical insurance coverage.
- Healthcare and dental costs
- Best retirement locations in Thailand
- Advice for single retiree

The book is also filled with cost comparison charts, helpful tips on living here and the best areas to live or retire in Thailand as an ex-pat.

A Retirees Guide to Southeast Asia: Cambodia, Vietnam, the Philippines and Laos

A Retirees Guide to South East Asia, Cambodia, Vietnam, The Philippines and Laos is the second book in The Retiree Series of travel books. The books are aimed at retirees or future retirees who want to enjoy their retirement years travelling and seeing places that they maybe couldn't afford or did not have time for when they were working and raising a family. Sixty-five is the new fifty so most of us are fitter and healthier than our parents were, and when you retire there is a whole world out there waiting for you to discover it. The challenge is being able to afford and enjoy your adventures on a pension. I am often amazed at some of the people I have spoken to on my travels who, have just booked their trip through a local travel agent, and not checked prices elsewhere. Though we may have travelled on the same aeroplane, gone on the same tour or been staying in the same hotel, the price I paid was sometimes half of what they had paid. I am not a backpacker, just a retiree who loves his comfort, staying in nice hotels, eating in good restaurants, drinking decent wine and cocktails and going on tours. I manage to do this on a retirement income by looking for bargains wherever and whenever I travel. This is a journal of a two-month trip that I took through Thailand, Cambodia, Vietnam, the Philippines and Laos. I did this trip on a budget, surviving on my pension. During that time I ticked off many items on my bucket list, ate and drank well, saw some breathtaking sights and did some amazing things including:

•The beauty of Angkor Wat and watching the sunrise over the temples.

•The atrocities of the Killing Fields and S_21 Prison in Phnom Phen.

•Sailed on the mighty Mekong River.

•Crawled through Vietnams Chu Chi Tunnels and visited the war museum.

•Explored the ancient cities of Ho Chi Min and Hanoi.

•Had clothing made to measure by expert tailors in Hoi An.

•Cruised Vietnams Halong Bay.

•Experienced Wind Surfing in Boracay and saw Bohol's Chocolate Hills in the Philippines.

•Visited Laos.

My philosophy is the more I can save when travelling, the more I can travel, having said that, be frugal, not cheap. Look for deals and don't waste money, but don't miss out on great experiences or walk miles to save money.

Same-Same But Different. Searching for the perfect place to retire in Thailand

There is a saying in Thailand: "Same same but different." I asked a Thai lady once what the meaning was and she answered "You and me the same, but different", which I think sums it up. It has become quite a catchphrase here in Thailand, and it is seen on tee shirts, and coffee mugs and heard all of the time, wherever you go. You might ask a local what's the best beer in Thailand, Chang, Leo or Singha? The answer would generally be "Same same but different", or what's the difference between Thai red curry and Thai green curry? "same same but different". So when I am asked what's it like retiring to and living in Thailand compared to Australia, England or the USA? My usual answer is, "same same but different", very different, very cheap and very enjoyable. Thailand is a magical place and I feel blessed that I can live here. Thailand is within easy reach of many other Southeast Asian countries by aeroplane, car or bus, and I travel to these areas and try to have new experiences whenever I can. Being a retiree I have to look after my money to make sure that it doesn't run out before I do, so I always travel within my means, on a budget, and with a plan.

It has been eighteen eventful months since I first arrived in Thailand to start my retirement. The time I have spent here has been full of highs and lows (mainly highs), and I know that I made the right decision to make Thailand my new home. It hasn't been easy, in fact, if you have already read my first book, The Retire in Thailand Handbook (The First Six Months) you would have seen that it was quite difficult to establish myself here and sometimes very frustrating and time-consuming. That was then and this is now. After the first six months, everything seemed to fall into place. I moved from Phuket to Koh Samui and rented a nice villa on the beach. I met and fell in love with a beautiful Thai lady, who is now my partner. This book starts where the last one left off, in Phuket and will take you on an exciting journey through Thailand, stopping off at many of the cities and towns expat retirees now call home. I decided to take the road trip to find the ideal town in Thailand to eventually settle down and call home. Thailand has so many beautiful places to choose from, tropical Islands, beach resorts, rural towns, farming towns, large bustling cities, and fishing villages. The choice of where you may want to live depends on your outlook on life and how you want to enjoy spending your new life once you have retired. As Thailand is 95% Buddhist a lot of the attractions around Thailand's rural and inland areas revolve around Buddhist temples, markets and national parks are also a big feature in rural Thailand. Bangkok, the coastal areas and the beautiful islands offer more entertainment, amusements, and nightlife, but if you want to see the real Thailand, not just Thailand that the tourist sees you should head to the heartland, to places like Chiang Mai, Chiang Rai, Nakhon Ratchasima, Udon Thani, and Khon Kaen.

Being on a pension, it was important for me to live within my means and within my budget, but I still wanted to be able to travel when I want to, and live my life to the fullest. To be able to do this and get the best deals you have to shop around. I am amazed at the people I have spoken to on my travels who have just booked their trip with a local travel agent, and not checked prices elsewhere. Though we may have travelled on the same aeroplane, gone on the same tour or be staying in the same hotel, the price I paid was sometimes half of what they had paid. This book will give you some great ideas on how you can save money when you travel, as well as an insight into great retirement areas within Thailand.

The way I look at it, the more you save the more you can travel and enjoy your life and your retirement.

A Retirees Guide to South East Asia. Myanmar, Singapore, Bali, and Malaysia

The Trouble With Retirement Is That You Never Get A Day Off.

Some people hate retirement, after fifty years of working most days of their lives, many find it hard to adjust to having so much time on their hands. I love being retired; my one regret is that I didn't have the money or the foresight to retire when I was younger. George Bernard Shaw said that "youth is wasted on the young", but for a lot of retirees "retirement is wasted on the old". They suddenly have all of this time (and sometimes money) on their hands and have no idea what to do with it. They end up going about their lives as they have always done, living in the same town, going to the same pub or club, staying home watching endless reality programs on the TV, basically watching other people living their lives, instead of living their own lives to the fullest. For me, retirement was an opportunity to do all of the things that I never had time to do while I was busy working and raising a family. In the two years I have been retired I have travelled extensively throughout the USA, the Caribbean and South East Asia, written three books, learnt to speak Thai (sort of), learned to windsurf (sort of), met and fell in love with a beautiful Thai lady, and I now live on the beautiful tropical island of Koh Samui in Thailand.

If you have read my third book "Same-Same but Different" in The Retirees Guide series of books, you will know that when I returned from my adventures in Cambodia, Vietnam, the Philippines and Laos (book two in the series), I settled back in Koh Samui. A few weeks after I returned from my trip, on Valentine's Day 2017, I met a beautiful girl called Jin. Within a few weeks of meeting, we were on an extended driving trip around Thailand. On our return from our Thailand road trip, we decided that we wanted to travel overseas for a month every year, to visit all of the countries we wanted to see together. Jin had never been out of Thailand before, and I wanted her to see some of the countries I had been fortunate enough to visit over the years, either on family holidays or when I was working at sea or in hotels around the world as a chef. We decided that for eleven months of the year, we would live on a budget that would still allow us to have a good life and travel around Thailand while saving up for our next overseas trip. This book is a journal of our first five-week overseas trip to Myanmar, Malaysia, Singapore and Bali, by road and air, train and sea. We stayed in some beautiful hotels, visited many local attractions, and ate in some fine restaurants well within the

The Ten Best Countries in The World To Retire On Your Pension

With 60 being the new 40 many retirees don't want to retire gracefully they want to retire disgracefully and have some fun in their lives while they still can. While researching my retiree travel books series, I have met retirees, who much to the dismay and sometimes disgust of their children and grandchildren, decided to move away from the comfort of their hometowns to start new lives far away in the mystical Far East and change their lives forever. One of them now rides a Harley Davidson motorbike, something that he had wanted to do since he was sixteen years old when he saw Peter Fonda ride one from

California to New Orleans in the movie "Easy Rider". Another retiree I interviewed was in his mid-60s and had married a 28-year-old bar lady, 14 months later she gave birth to a baby girl and he was loving the responsibility of being a father for the very first time...and yes, they were very happy together. Another retiree I talked with had bought a sailing boat and learned how to sail at the age of 63 (41 in new year's) and now spends his time sailing around South-East Asia. You don't have to go to those extremes, but if you have secretly longed to do something different in your life while you were working and raising a family now is the time to do it...you don't want to die wondering what might have been.

You may be retiring soon or maybe you have already retired after working hard all of your life and you will have the time and money to live your life to the fullest. Well, you hope that you will have enough money to live your life to the fullest. Many people that have retired or are retiring had well-paying jobs, a healthy superannuation account, invested wisely and saved enough money to live out their retirement years in comparative luxury. Unfortunately, many more retirees have not been so lucky or so foresighted and only have their government retirement pension and whatever savings and investments they have managed to accumulate over their working lives, and for them, the thought of living in retirement can sometimes be quite scary.

For those retirees, retiring to an overseas country has become a real consideration, because they can spend a lot less money, and get a whole lot more due to the lower cost of living than they would be able to by staying in their home countries. Add to this the tempting incentives of tropical climates and exciting new experiences to spice up your life and you can see why more and more retirees from all over the world are looking for alternative retirement options abroad. This book lists the ten best countries in the world for retirees to live where they can enjoy their retirement to the fullest on their pensions.

• Thailand
• Malaysia

- Vietnam
- Bali
- Cambodia
- Spain
- Portugal
- Costa Rica
- Belize
- Panama

The ten countries are all waiting to welcome you; it will be up to you to decide which is the best country that suits your circumstances.

BIOGRAPHY

You will never amount to anything.: One man's journey through life to prove that his teacher was wrong

When I was four years old, my mum took me and my brother to Jamaica to join my dad who had been transferred from London to work in Kingston Town as a foreman scaffolder on a twelve month contract. There began my love affair with island life, sea, sand and surf. A few years later, when we came back to the UK we moved to Middlesbrough in north east England, my dad's home town. We went from living like royalty, on a sun-drenched island, surrounded by palm trees, clear blue seas and golden beaches, to living in impoverished conditions in a cold, colourless northern town, with steelworks and two chemical plants polluting the air with noxious gasses. I made a promise to myself then that I was going to get out of that town and get back to Jamaica or some other island or country where there were happy smiling faces, blue seas, parrots, beaches and sunshine as soon as I possibly could. The day I left school for the last time, was the day the school broke up for the Easter holidays. The headmaster had decided that the few pupils who were not staying on to do their CSE or GCSE exams and who were leaving school for good on that day, should leave at lunch time. There were only six of us and we were escorted from the school grounds by one of the teachers. When we were approaching the school gates, I heard a voice from behind yelling "You lot will never amount to anything, you'll all end up as drunks, unemployed or in prison" I recognised the voice straight away, it was Mr Bagley, my science teacher, who had bullied, tormented and beaten me at every opportunity over the past four years. That just made me more determined to get away from England and start a new life in the tropics. His words have stayed with me to this day, and they have given me the strength to prove him wrong. I have had to cheat, lie and live by my wits to achieve my goals but since that day I have never looked back. I have worked as a chef on cruise ships, five star hotels and restaurants around the world, been to the Antarctic, lived in ten different countries, own four investment properties and a share portfolio, had my own successful advertising business, own a beautiful house on the Gold Coast in Australia, own a boat in Boracay in the Philippines, wrote and had a book published on how to retire in Thailand, and I now live on the beautiful island of Koh Samui in the Gulf of Thailand.

My life's been fantastic Mr Bagley. How about yours?

The Deptford Mask Murders: The First Capital Murder Trial in 1905 Using Fingerprint Forensics

In 1905 a crime took place in London that would change the way that police forces around the world would identify criminal suspects, the Deptford Mask Murders.

On the 27th of March 1905, Thomas Farrow was found beaten to death in an oil and paint shop he managed in Deptford. Ann Farrow, Thomas's wife was also badly beaten and succumbed to her injuries and died in hospital one week later. This was the crime that the Scotland Yard Fingerprint Bureau had been waiting for since the bureau was formed in 1901, a high profile crime that would put the spotlight on the science of fingerprinting as a reliable, efficient and infallible system of identifying criminals.

A week after the crime was committed; Brothers Alfred and Albert Stratton were arrested and were later put on trial at the Old Bailey accused of wilful murder. The prosecution had very little evidence to convict the brothers and what they did have was mainly circumstantial, except for a thumbprint which was found on a cash box in the Farrows bedroom above the paint shop. Fingerprinting had never been used to solve a serious crime before in Britain and was often seen as being untrustworthy and untested, with one magistrate writing to The Times; "Scotland Yard, once known as the world's finest police organisation, will be the laughing stock of Europe it if insists on trying to trace criminals by odd ridges on their skins." The book is based on those true events and is my interpretation of what I believe could have happened 115 years ago when fingerprints were used for the very first time in Great Britain to convict the Stratton brothers of willful murder.

All of the main characters in this book who played their part in having the brothers convicted were real people in this extraordinary historical event.

FICTION

Adolf Fittler

This book is a work of fiction, though it's based on my own experiences when growing up In Middlesbrough during the1960sThis was the time of the Windrush era when immigrants from the Caribbean came to the UK, to undertake a variety of jobs to help rebuild the nation. After WWII. The book takes in the difficulties that the immigrants faced due to their ethnicity and the colour of their skin.

My dad, John Fittler was a racist as was his father before him. Dad always said, to anyone who would listen, that if he had been born in Alabama or Mississippi in the USA, he would have been in the Klu Klux Klan, burning crosses and lynching niggers. Unfortunately for him, he was born in Middlesbrough in the county of Yorkshire in England. I started my life as a racist; I had little choice, as growing up that was all that my father talked about, every conversation always seemed to revolve around or relate to black or Asian people. After the Second World War black and ethnic minorities from Commonwealth countries were now starting to arrive in Britain, driving buses, working in the shops, or working on building sites building new housing estates in the town, there were even two Pakistanis working on the docks, though thankfully not alongside my dad as they worked on the opposite shift to him. Some immigrants who arrived in the country with some money decided to go into business and opened up shops, restaurants, or other businesses. I had little to do with any immigrants, the ones that were in our school I avoided, as did most of the other white kids in the school and the black and Asian kids tended to stick together as there was safety in numbers. In June 1959 there was a turning point in my life, an event that would transform the way that I would view the world and live my life when Winston and Kaleisha Brown, two kids from Jamaica moved into a council house on Granville Street in the Cannon Street area of town, just two doors down from the Fittler house.

FEATURING LIEUTENT CHAI SON SINUAN AN INCORRUPTIBLE POLICE OFFICER IN A POLICE FORCE RIFE WITH CORRUPTION

Thai Died, Murder in Paradise: Corona Has Come To Kho Samui But So Has Another Killer

On the Paradise Island of Koh Samui a young English girl's body is found posed looking out to sea on Bophut Beach. Her throat has been cut to near decapitation and Police Lieutenant Chai Son Sinuan of the Royal Thailand Police is handed the toughest murder case of his career. At the same time, Covid-19 has devastated Koh Samui's and Thailand's tourist industry and the government is putting pressure on Son to solve the case to save face with the international community. Son is in a race against time to solve the murder, but with most businesses, hotels, massage parlours, restaurants and bars now closed and with many potential witnesses having already left the island to return to their home countries or provinces around Thailand there are very few leads to follow. The investigation takes Son to Ko Pha-Ngan and to the Island of Phuket and then back to Koh Samui as he untangles a crime with links back to the notorious gangsters the Kray twins the most feared, most ruthless gangsters in London during the 1950s and 1960s.

Thai Died...Bar Girl

On the tropical island of Koh Samui, a bar girl has gone missing. The granddaughter of a high ranking General with connections to the upper echelons of the Thai army government has also gone missing and Police Lieutenant Chai Son Sinuan of the Royal Thailand Police, an incorruptible policeman in a police force that is deeply rooted in corruption is assigned the case. As Son starts his investigation the bar girl's mutilated body is found and then two more bar girls go missing. To make matters worse a German resident of Koh Samui, who is the younger brother of a government minister in the Christian Democratic Union party in the German Bundestag went for his usual afternoon bike ride two days before and he has not been seen since. As Son learns more about the missing German and the general's granddaughter, he is convinced that the investigations are connected. The clock is ticking and Son is in a race against time to solve the crimes before the killer strikes again. The story takes the reader to the hard-core red light districts of Koh Samui, where girls from poor villages in rural areas of Thailand come to work in the lady bars to try to support their families by selling themselves to the "farang" who come from all corners of the world to take full advantage of the girl's troubled lives.

Thai Died...Lawyers Guns and Money

On the tranquil shores of Crystal Bay on the tropical island of Koh Samui, a woman's body floats to shore on the afternoon tide. Unnoticed, she drifts close to the many tourists taking advantage of the tepid water to try to cool down in the hot mid-afternoon sun. She is naked except for a Buddhist amulet around one of her wrists and a silk scarf tied tightly around her neck and she has distinctive Sak Yant tattoos down her back. It looked like a straightforward case of a bar girl taking the wrong customer home for the night until a phone call to the police station from an expat husband in Bangkok saying that his wife a high-profile prosecutor had not been answering her phone since the previous evening and that he had contacted the management at their holiday home on the island to check on her when he had entered the house he found an overturned coffee table drops of blood on the broken glass but no sign of his wife.

After the woman's body is identified as the missing prosecutor, it comes to light that she was building a case against a Russian drug cartel boss operating out of Phuket with links to the Asian underworld.

When pressure from the upper echelons of the Thai government works its way down to the police minister, he contacts Colonel Chief Superintendent Saetang and demands that he make a quick arrest. Knowing that his best investigator had been banished to Koh Phangan, Colonel Saetang recalls Lieutenant Chai Son Sinuan from his exile back to Koh Samui to try to solve the case.

NOTES

NOTES

Printed in Great Britain
by Amazon